Informing the legislative debate since 1914 _____

Next Steps in Nuclear Arms Control with Russia: Issues for Congress

Amy F. Woolf
Specialist in Nuclear Weapons Policy

January 6, 2014

Congressional Research Service

7-5700

www.crs.gov

R43037

Summary

In his 2013 State of the Union Address, President Obama stated that the United States would "engage Russia to seek further reductions in our nuclear arsenals." These reductions could include limits on strategic, nonstrategic and nondeployed nuclear weapons. Yet, arms control negotiations between the United States and Russia have stalled, leading many observers to suggest that the United States reduce its nuclear forces unilaterally, or in parallel with Russia, without negotiating a new treaty. Many in Congress have expressed concerns about this possibility, both because they question the need to reduce nuclear forces below New START levels and because they do not want the President to agree to further reductions without seeking the approval of Congress.

Over the years, the United States reduced its nuclear weapons with formal, bilateral treaties, reciprocal, but informal, understandings, and unilateral adjustments to its force posture. The role of Congress in the arms control process depends on the mechanism used to reduce forces. If the United States and Russia sign a formal treaty, then the Senate must signal its advice and consent with a vote of two-thirds of its Members. The House and Senate would each need to pass legislation approving an Executive Agreement. But the President can reduce U.S. nuclear weapons in parallel with Russia, without seeking congressional approval, if the reductions are taken unilaterally, or as the result of a nonbinding political agreement.

Each of the mechanisms for reducing nuclear forces can possess different characteristics for the arms control process. These include balance and equality, predictability, flexibility, transparency and confidence in compliance, and timeliness. Provisions in formal treaties can mandate balance and equality between the two sides' forces. They can also provide both sides with the ability to predict the size and structure of the other's current and future forces. Unilateral measures allow each side to maintain flexibility in deciding the size and structure of its nuclear forces. In addition, the monitoring and verification provisions included in bilateral treaties can provide each side with detailed information about the numbers and capabilities of the other's nuclear forces, while also helping each side confirm that the other has complied with the limits and restrictions in the treaty. With unilateral reductions, the two sides could still agree to share information, or they could withhold information so that they would not have to share sensitive data about their forces.

It usually takes far longer to reduce nuclear forces through a bilateral arms control treaty than it takes to adopt unilateral adjustments to nuclear forces. The need to find balanced and equitable trades, limits acceptable to both sides, detailed definitions of systems limited by the treaty, and agreed procedures for monitoring and verification can slow the process of negotiations. In addition, it can take months or years for a treaty to enter into force, both because the legislatures must review and vote on the treaty and because other domestic or international events intervene. In contrast, the nations may be able to adopt and implement unilateral adjustments more quickly.

If the Obama Administration reduces U.S. nuclear forces in parallel with Russia, but without a formal treaty, the two nations could avoid months or years in negotiations. Because New START would remain in force, predictability and transparency would remain important. Balance and equality would, however, receive a lower priority, while flexibility and timeliness would grow more important. Congress may question whether such an agreement is subject to congressional review. It may also seek to limit funding for further reductions through the annual authorization and appropriations process if it does not support the Administration's approach to further reductions. This report will be updated as needed.

Contents

Tables

Contacts

Introduction

On January 31, 2013, during the Senate Armed Services Committee's hearing on the nomination of former Senator Chuck Hagel to be Secretary of Defense, Senator Jeff Sessions questioned Senator Hagel about the Obama Administration's plans for the next steps in nuclear arms control.[1] Specifically, he asked Senator Hagel whether he was committed to honoring the provision in the FY2013 National Defense Authorization Act (P.L. 112-239, Section 1282) that requires the Administration to provide briefings to Congress, twice each year, on the status of arms control negotiations with Russia. Senator Hagel responded that he was committed to pursuing the required consultations. Senator Sessions then asked Senator Hagel for a commitment that the Administration would pursue agreements that would lead to further reductions in U.S. nuclear weapons through "the treaty-making power of the President." Specifically, he was seeking assurances that the Obama Administration would not try to bypass the Senate, and its role in providing advice and consent to the ratification of treaties, by reducing U.S. nuclear weapons through unilateral or informal bilateral means. Senator Hagel did not respond to this request. He noted that the President "believes in and is committed to treaties," but he did not accept Senator Sessions' view that future reductions in U.S. nuclear weapons should occur only through the treaty-making process.

Senator Sessions' questions, and the concerns voiced by other Members of Congress, respond to both the Obama Administration's stated interest in pursuing further reductions in nuclear weapons and indications in some press reports that the Administration may pursue these reductions, as President George H.W. Bush did in 1991, without a formal treaty.[2] President Obama views New START, which was signed by the United States and Russia in April 2010 and entered into force in February 2011,[3] as "just one step on a longer journey."[4] In his State of the Union Address on February 12, 2013, he pledged that "America will continue to lead the effort to prevent the spread of the world's most dangerous weapons." As a part of this effort, the United States would "engage Russia to seek further reductions in our nuclear arsenals."[5]

The United States and Russia have not yet started formal negotiations on further reductions in nuclear weapons. Disagreements about a number of issues, including the U.S. interest in limiting nonstrategic nuclear weapons and Russia's interest in limiting U.S. ballistic missile defense programs, have contributed to this delay. At the same time, congressional concerns about both the Administration's plans to reduce further U.S. nuclear warheads and the magnitude of the Administration's funding requests for the modernization of the U.S. nuclear enterprise have raised questions about whether the Senate would consent to ratification of a new treaty. As a result, many analysts and officials have suggested that the United States and Russia pursue "parallel

---

[1] U.S. Congress, Senate Armed Services, *Nomination of Former Senator Chuck Hagel to be Secretary of Defense*, Hearing, 113th Cong., 1st sess., January 31, 2013.

[2] See, for example, the comments of Senators Bob Corker and Jim Inofe in ""Nuclear Zero" Offers Nothing worth Having," *Wall Street Journal*, February 26, 2013, p. A15.

[3] For information about this treaty see CRS Report R41219, *The New START Treaty: Central Limits and Key Provisions*, by Amy F. Woolf

[4] The White House. Office of the Press Secretary. Remarks on Signing the Strategic Arms Reduction Treaty With President Dmitry A. Medvedev of Russia and an Exchange With Reporters in Prague, Czech Republic, April 8, 2010 http://www.gpo.gov/fdsys/pkg/DCPD-201000241/pdf/DCPD-201000241.pdf.

[5] The White House. Office of the Press Secretary. Remarks by the President in the State of the Union Address, February 12, 2013. http://www.whitehouse.gov/the-press-office/2013/02/12/remarks-president-state-union-address.

reductions" based on a mutual understanding, rather than a formal treaty.[6] Press reports indicate that the Administration is considering this approach and might seek an informal understanding, within the framework of the New START Treaty, that reduces current negotiated limits on U.S. and Russian forces.[7]

Over the years, the United States has used three mechanisms to reduce its nuclear weapons—formal, bilateral treaties; reciprocal, but informal, understandings; and unilateral adjustments to its force posture. Each of these mechanisms for reducing forces serves different purposes, and each can possess different characteristics for the arms control process. The role of Congress in the arms control process also depends on the mechanism used to reduce forces.

The United States signed several formal arms control treaties that limited the numbers of deployed nuclear weapons with the Soviet Union during the Cold War and with Russia in the past two decades.[8] Following Article II of the Constitution, the Senate reviewed these treaties, and, in most cases, voted to provide its advice and consent to ratification. The United States has also reduced its forces unilaterally, with reciprocity from Russia in 1991, when President George H.W. Bush withdrew and eliminated most U.S. shorter range nonstrategic nuclear weapons from bases in Europe and Asia. President Bush did not notify Congress or seek congressional approval before pursuing these reductions.[9] President George W. Bush also withdrew from deployment a number of U.S. nonstrategic nuclear weapons, although he did so without seeking or expecting reciprocity from Russia. He also pursued these reductions without seeking approval from Congress. Several Presidents have reduced unilaterally the number of warheads in the U.S. stored stockpile, as the United States has retired older weapons and responded to changing assessments of the necessary size and structure of the U.S. nuclear force. These changes are a part of the normal force planning process, managed by the Department of Defense and approved by the President, and have also occurred without prior explicit approval from Congress.

This report reviews these characteristics and demonstrates their effect on decisions about the use of the different mechanisms. The report begins with a review of the role of nuclear arms control in the U.S.-Soviet relationship, looking at both formal, bilateral treaties and unilateral steps the United States took to alter its nuclear posture. It then turns to the role of arms control in the U.S.-Russian relationship, again reviewing the role of both formal treaties and unilateral measures. The report also describes the role of Congress in the arms control process. It then provides an analytic framework that reviews the characteristics of the different mechanisms, focusing on issues such as balance and equality, predictability, flexibility, transparency and confidence in compliance, and

---

[6] International Security Advisory Board, *Options for Implementing Additional Nuclear Force Reductions*, United States Department of State, Report, Washington, DC, November 27, 2012, p. 5. http://www.state.gov/documents/organization/201403.pdf.

[7] R. Jeffrey Smith, "Obama Embraces Big Nuke Cuts," *Foreign Policy*, February 8, 2013. http://www.foreignpolicy.com/articles/2013/02/08/obama_embraces_big_nuke_cuts. See, also, Peter Baker and David E. Sanger, "Obama Has Plans to Cut U.S. Nuclear Arsenal, if Russia Reciprocates," *New York Times*, July 18, 2013. http://www.nytimes.com/2013/06/19/world/obama-has-plans-to-cut-us-nuclear-arsenal-if-russia-reciprocates.html?hp&_r=1&.

[8] For a brief summary of the each of these agreements, see CRS Report RL33865, *Arms Control and Nonproliferation: A Catalog of Treaties and Agreements*, by Amy F. Woolf, Paul K. Kerr, and Mary Beth D. Nikitin.

[9] President Bush was prepared to move forward with the reductions, which came to be known as the Presidential Nuclear Initiatives (PNIs), even if the Soviet Union did not alter its force posture. For a summary of the process leading up to the PNIs, and the content of the initiatives, see Susan J. Koch, *The Presidential Nuclear Initiatives of 1991-1992*, Center for the Study of Weapons of Mass Destruction, National Defense University, Case Study Series, Washington, DC, September 2012. http://www.ndu.edu/press/lib/pdf/CSWMD-CaseStudy/CSWMD_CaseStudy-5.pdf.

timeliness. Finally the report describes issues that Congress may address as the Obama Administration employs these mechanisms to pursue further reductions in U.S. nuclear weapons.

This report does not address the question of whether the United States should pursue further reductions in deployed nuclear weapons, or, if it does, how deep those reductions should be. While many in Congress disagree with the Administration's plans for further reductions, that goal is its stated policy. As a result, the report evaluates different mechanisms that the Administration might use to implement that policy without questioning the underlying policy. In addition, the report will evaluate these mechanisms only in the context of reductions in U.S. and Russian nuclear weapons. It will not evaluate whether other nations—such as China, the United Kingdom, and France—should participate in these reductions or which mechanism would be appropriate if other nations did participate. The United States and Russia deploy far greater numbers of nuclear weapons than these other nations,[10] so they may be able to reduce their weapons further before bringing other nations into the process.

The Changing Role of Nuclear Arms Control

Limits and Reductions During the Cold War

Formal Treaties and Agreements

During the Cold War, before the demise of the Soviet Union at the end of 1991, arms control played a key role in the relationship between the United States and Soviet Union. Between 1972 and 1991, the two nations signed four treaties and one executive agreement that limited offensive nuclear weapons and ballistic missile defenses.[11] As **Table 1** indicates, all but one of these treaties entered into force.

Arms control negotiations were often one of the few channels for formal communication between the two nations. The talks provided the United States and Soviet Union with a forum to air their security concerns and raise questions about their plans and programs. Over time, the discussions during negotiations and the data and access mandated by the monitoring provisions included in the treaties allowed for a measure of transparency about the numbers and capabilities of current forces. As the volume of shared information grew over the years, each side could replace suspicions about the intentions of the other with confidence in its understanding of the capabilities of the other's nuclear forces. The limits also helped each side predict and plan for the future size and shape of the other's forces. To most observers, this process reduced the risk of nuclear war and strengthened U.S. security. It helped both sides avoid worst-case assumptions about the future that could fuel an arms race or undermine stability.

---

[10] Under New START, the United States and Russia will deploy 1,550 strategic warheads. According to unclassified estimates, France deploys around 300 warheads, China around 240 warheads, and the United Kingdom around 160 warheads.

[11] For information about limits in these treaties and agreements, see CRS Report RL33865, *Arms Control and Nonproliferation: A Catalog of Treaties and Agreements*, by Amy F. Woolf, Paul K. Kerr, and Mary Beth D. Nikitin.

Table 1. U.S.-Soviet Arms Control Agreements
1972-1991

Treaty/Agreement	Year	Format	Status
ABM Treaty	1972	Treaty	Entered into force in 1972; lapsed after U.S. withdrawal in 2002
SALT I Interim Agreement	1972	Executive Agreement	Entered into force in 1972, due to remain in force for 5 years
SALT II	1979	Treaty	Did not enter into force
INF	1987	Treaty	Entered into force in 1988; reductions complete in 1991; remains in force
START	1991	Treaty	Entered into force in 1994; reductions complete in 2001; lapsed in December 2009

Others, however, questioned the value of these talks. Some argued that the agreements merely codified existing force structure plans and restricted the U.S. ability to respond to emerging threats. For example, during the 1980s, when the United States renewed its interest and expanded its research into extensive land-based and space-based defenses against ballistic missiles, the 1972 Anti-ballistic Missile (ABM) Treaty continued to limit it to 100 interceptors deployed at one specific location. Some also questioned whether the Soviet Union would comply with its obligations, as the monitoring process revealed evidence of activities that were inconsistent with expectations under the treaties.[12] In spite of predictions to the contrary, however, there was little evidence that the Soviet Union sought to evade the limits in the treaties in any systematic way.[13] Instead, many of the concerns derived from ambiguities in the terms of the treaties and most were resolved in discussions held in compliance review commissions established by the treaties.

The United States and Soviet Union also used arms control negotiations, and the resulting treaties, as a way to limit or reduce the specific weapons systems that they viewed as threatening and destabilizing.[14] For example, during the late 1970s and early 1980s, the Soviet Union deployed intermediate range missiles that could reach critical targets in NATO. The United States responded by deploying intermediate-range missiles in Europe; these could have reached

---

[12] The U.S. State Department issued numerous reports about Soviet (and Russian) activities that appeared inconsistent with arms control obligations. For recent reports, see http://www.state.gov/t/avc/rls/rpt/c54051 htm.

[13] Many observers cite the Soviet construction of a large early warning radar at Krasnoyarsk as evidence of Soviet intent to violate not only the ABM Treaty, but also arm control agreements in general. The building for this radar was constructed in central Siberia, facing northeast across the country, rather than on the periphery facing out, as mandated by the ABM Treaty. The Soviet Union claimed it was a space-track radar, and, therefore, not limited by the ABM Treaty, but, in the late 1980s, it did agree to dismantle the facility before it became operational. Most experts agree that it was probably an early warning radar, and was located in Krasnoyarsk for the sake of convenience and proximity to the trans-Siberian railway. Nevertheless, its location was inconsistent with the terms of the ABM Treaty.

[14] For a discussion of the relationship between arms control negotiations and efforts to limit weapons that were viewed as destabilizing, see Michael S. Gerson, "The Origins of Strategic Stability: the United States and the threat of Surprise Attack," in Elbridge A. Colby and Michael S. Gerson, *Strategic Stability: Contending Interpretations* (Carlisle, PA: Strategic Studies Institute and U.S. Army War College Press, 2013), p. 35.

---

leadership and command and control targets in the Soviet Union in less than 10 minutes. Some analysts feared that these weapons would provide the United States and NATO with the ability to "decapitate" Soviet leadership, thereby giving NATO an incentive to use these weapons early in a conflict and the Soviets an incentive to launch its forces quickly before it lost the ability to control its nuclear operations.[15] With both sides fearing a first strike from the other, each had an incentive to reduce the threat. As a result, they negotiated the 1987 Intermediate-range Nuclear Forces (INF) Treaty, which eliminated all intermediate-range nuclear missiles.[16]

In a similar vein, throughout the Cold War, U.S. analysts expressed concerns about the Soviet force of large "heavy" intercontinental ballistic missiles (ICBMs) that could often carry multiple warheads (known as multiple independently-targeted reentry-vehicles—MIRVs.) Analysts feared that the Soviet Union might consider using these weapons in a "disarming" first strike against U.S. ICBMs based in fixed, vulnerable, land-based silos. Moreover, because these Soviet missiles were also deployed in fixed, vulnerable, land-based silos, the Soviet Union might feel pressure to launch them early in a crisis, before it lost them to a U.S. strike. The United States sought to mitigate concerns about the vulnerability of its own forces by deploying many of its warheads at sea, on invulnerable submarine-launched ballistic missiles (SLBMs). But it also sought to limit and reduce the numbers of large ICBMs in the Soviet force through arms control agreements. Initially, in the 1970s Strategic Arms Limitation Talks (SALT), it sought to cap the numbers of permitted missiles. In the 1991 Strategic Arms Reduction Treaty (START), the Soviet Union agreed to reduce these weapons by 50%. And in the 1993 START II Treaty, Russia agreed to eliminate all these missiles.[17]

Unilateral Adjustments

The bilateral treaties between the United States and Soviet Union did not contain any limits or restrictions on shorter-range nuclear weapons, which are often referred to as tactical or nonstrategic nuclear weapons. Both nations were free to adjust the numbers, types, and deployment areas for these weapons according to their own assessments of the forces needed to assure their national security. These treaties also did not limit the numbers of extra warheads that either side could retain in storage, in a "nondeployed" stockpile. Each nation was also free to determine, for itself, how many spare warheads it needed and how and when to add these warheads to its deployed forces.

Nonstrategic Nuclear Weapons[18]

Throughout the Cold War, the United States deployed nonstrategic nuclear weapons at U.S. bases in Asia and on the territories of several NATO allies in Europe. The United States often altered

---

[15] For a discussion of the Soviet fear of decapitation, see David Hoffman, *Dead Hand: The Untold Story of the Cold War Arms Race and its Dangerous Legacy* (New York: Doubleday, 2009), pp. 145-152.

[16] For information about the INF Treaty, see CRS Report RL33865, *Arms Control and Nonproliferation: A Catalog of Treaties and Agreements*, by Amy F. Woolf, Paul K. Kerr, and Mary Beth D. Nikitin, pp. 7-8.

[17] Because START II never entered into force, Russia still deploys large, MIRVed ICBMs. Reports also indicate that it plans to develop and deploy, later this decade, a new heavy MIRVed ICBM to replace the aging missiles deployed in the 1980s. For details, see "Russia to Develop New Heavy ICBM by 2020," *Ria Novosti*, December 20, 2010. http://en rian ru/russia/20101220/161856876 html.

[18] For a detailed review of U.S. nonstrategic nuclear weapons, see CRS Report RL32572, *Nonstrategic Nuclear Weapons*, by Amy F. Woolf.

the size and structure of these forces in response to changing capabilities and changing threat assessments. It began to reduce these forces in the late 1970s, with the number of deployed warheads declining from more than 7,000 in the mid-1970s to below 6,000 in the mid-1980s.[19] These reductions occurred, for the most part, because U.S. and NATO officials believed they could maintain deterrence with fewer, but more modern, weapons. For example, when the NATO allies agreed in 1970 that the United States should deploy new intermediate-range nuclear weapons in Europe, they decided to remove 1,000 older nuclear weapons from Europe. And in 1983, in the Montebello Decision, when the NATO defense ministers approved additional weapons modernization plans, they also called for a further reduction of 1,400 nonstrategic nuclear weapons.[20] The Pentagon implemented these reductions as a part of its regular force planning process; it did not seek or need the approval of Congress.

The number of U.S. nonstrategic nuclear weapons dropped sharply in the waning days of the Cold War, falling to fewer than 1,000 warheads by the mid-1990s, as a result of an initiative, now known as the Presidential Nuclear Initiative (PNI), announced in 1991 by President George H.W. Bush. Under this initiative, the United States withdrew from deployment more than 2,000 land-based and sea-based nonstrategic nuclear weapons. President Bush indicated that the United States would take these steps unilaterally, and would implement these measures regardless of the Soviet reaction. The Pentagon indicated that the steps represented "sound military policy" regardless of the Soviet reaction.[21] In addition, President Bush identified and adopted these steps without consulting with or notifying Congress.[22] According to some reports, the "legislative strategy" never came up during meetings in the Pentagon.[23] Congress, for the most part, did not object to the reductions or insist that the United States wait for Soviet reciprocity before acting. To the contrary, several Members suggested that the United States could cut other nuclear programs and reduce its forces further.[24]

Nondeployed weapons

The United States maintains a stockpile of warheads in storage that are not deployed with operational delivery systems. Many of these warheads are awaiting dismantlement, but some remain active and could return to the force to replace warheads removed for maintenance or to add to the deployed force if warranted by changes in the international security environment. The size of this stockpile has declined sharply over the decades as the United States has reduced its

[19] *Toward a Nuclear Peace: The Future of Nuclear Weapons in U.S. Foreign and Defense Policy,*, Report of the CSIS Nuclear Strategy Study Group, Washington, DC, 1993, p. 27.

[20] The text of the Montebello Decision can be found in Jeffrey A. Larson and Kurt J. Klingenberger, *Controlling Non-strategic Nuclear Weapons: Obstacles and Opportunities* (Colorado Springs, CO: Institute for National Security Studies, 2001), pp. 265-266.

[21] Helen Dewar and Barton Gelman, "Bush Administration Signals Flexibilty on Additional Cuts in Nuclear Weapons," *Washington Post*, October 1, 1991, p. A16. The Bush Administration challenged the Soviet Union to take similar steps, and on October 5, 1991, Soviet President Mikhail Gorbachev replied, stating that he would also withdraw and eliminate nonstrategic nuclear weapons. Susan J. Koch, *The Presidential Nuclear Initiatives of 1991-1992*, Center for the Study of Weapons of Mass Destruction, National Defense University, Case Study Series, Washington, DC, September 2012, p. 8. http://www.ndu.edu/press/lib/pdf/CSWMD-CaseStudy/CSWMD_CaseStudy-5.pdf.

[22] See, for example, the comments of Senator Albert Gore, "Nuclear Weapons," Remarks, *Congressional Record*, October 7, 1991, p. S14468.

[23] Helen Dewar and Barton Gelman, "Bush Administration Signals Flexibilty on Additional Cuts in Nuclear Weapons," *Washington Post*, October 1, 1991, p. A16.

[24] Dan Balz, "Democrats, on Defensive, Press Home-Front Theme," *Washington Post*, September 29, 1991, p. A38.

numbers of deployed warheads, retired many types of Cold War-era systems, and reduced its requirements for spare warheads. According to a fact sheet released by the Obama Administration in May 2010, the stockpile reached its maximum level of 31,255 warheads in 1967.[25] It declined to a total of 23,205 warheads in 1988, the year before the Warsaw Pact dissolved. During the George H.W. Bush Administration, reductions accelerated, with the total declining nearly 40%, from 22,217 warheads in 1989 to 13,708 warheads in 1992.

The United States and Soviet Union never counted these warheads under the limits in arms control treaties. As a result, the United States has implemented all of the reductions in its stockpile unilaterally. These reductions occurred as the United States retired and dismantled warheads removed from older delivery systems, as it replaced older types of warheads with new types, and as it altered its assessment of the number of warheads needed to maintain and augment the deployed force. They followed not only the implementation of the PNIs, but also reflected further changes that the United States made in its nuclear strategy and targeting doctrine in response to the changing international security environment. While Congress often debated plans for the missiles and bombers that would deliver U.S. nuclear weapons and reviewed administration plans to design or tests new types of warheads, it rarely questioned or discussed the size of the stockpile of spare warheads.

Limits and Reductions After the Cold War

Formal Treaties and Agreements

During the 1990s, as the relationship between the United States and Russia improved, their cooperation expanded to include a wide range of economic, political, and military issues. As a result, arms control negotiations no longer played a central role in fostering cooperation between the two nations. Nevertheless, as **Table 2**, below, indicates, the United States and Russia have negotiated three arms control treaties since 1992. Two of these have entered into force.

The United States and Russia negotiated a second Strategic Arms Reduction Treaty (START II) in 1992 (they signed it in early January 1993) both to implement further reductions in their forces and to "enhance strategic stability and predictability."[26] The Treaty, if it had entered into force, would have reduced the number of deployed strategic warheads to 3,500, banned multiple warhead ICBMs, which the United States considered destabilizing in a crisis, and limited the number of warheads on SLBMs, which Russia believed the United States could use in a pre-emptive first strike.[27]

---

[25] Department of Energy, "Increasing Transparency in the U.S. Nuclear Stockpile," Fact Sheet. May 3, 2010, p. 1. http://www.defense.gov/npr/docs/10-05-03_Fact_Sheet_US_Nuclear_Transparency__FINAL_w_Date.pdf. When the fact sheet was released in May 2010, the size of the stockpile stood at 5,113 warheads. According to recent unclassified estimates it has declined further, to approximately 4,688 warheads in early 2013. see Hans M. Kristensen, (Still) Secret U.S. Nuclear Weapons Stockpile Reduced. FAS Strategic Security Blog, February 26, 2013. http://www.fas.org/blog/ssp/2013/02/stockpilereduction.php.

[26] Preamble to the Treaty Between the United States of America and the Russian Federation on Further Reduction and Limitation of Strategic Offensive Arms (START II). http://www.state.gov/t/avc/trty/102887 htm#treatytext

[27] As is noted in more detail below, a number of issues related to both the treaty and the U.S.-Russian relationship stalled START II ratification. The two nations eventually replaced it with the 2002 Moscow Treaty.

Table 2. U.S.-Russian Arms Control Treaties

1992-2013

Treaty/ Agreement	Year	Format	Status
START II	1993	Treaty	Did not enter into force
Moscow Treaty (SORT)	2002	Treaty	Entered into force in 2003; would have lapsed in 2012, but lapsed on EIF of New START
New START	2010	Treaty	Entered into force in 2011

The United States and Russia did not sign any bilateral strategic arms control treaties during the Clinton Administration, although they did work together to implement START I, sharing data and cooperating on a range of on-site inspections. They also sought to reach agreement on further reductions, in a START III Treaty, which might have reduced their strategic forces to 2,500 deployed warheads, but the two governments failed to conclude the negotiations before the end of the Clinton Administration.

During the 1990s, many analysts inside and outside government grew convinced that the United States no longer needed arms control to limit the Russian threat. They expected Russian forces to decline sharply, under economic pressure, as Russia retired older systems without producing large numbers of new weapons. Therefore, they believed that United States would not need to limit its own forces in an effort to convince Russia to reduce its arsenal. Furthermore, other nations, such as those seeking their own nuclear weapons and those armed with chemical and biological weapons, seemed to pose new threats to U.S. national security. Many analysts opposed further reductions in U.S. nuclear weapons because they believed nuclear weapons might help deter these new and emerging threats.

During the election campaign in 2000 and his early months in office in 2001, President George W. Bush pledged to set aside the arms control negotiating process and to reduce U.S. strategic nuclear forces unilaterally, to the "lowest possible number consistent with our national security." He did not think that a formal, bilateral treaty was necessary to implement these reductions; instead he indicated that "we can and will change the size, the composition, the character of our nuclear forces in a way that reflects the reality that the Cold War is over."[28] The Bush Administration indicated that the size and structure of Russia's nuclear arsenal would no longer affect U.S. nuclear plans and programs, and as a result, the United States no longer needed the predictability offered by the limits in arms control agreements.

The Bush Administration also saw no reason to pursue arms control negotiations to manage the U.S. relationship with Russia. To the contrary, Administration officials argued that formal arms control negotiations represented an adversarial process between the United States and Russia and they were no longer appropriate because, according to the President and others in his Administration, "Russia is no longer our enemy."[29] Accordingly, the Bush Administration

---

[28] News Event. George W. Bush, President of the United States, Delivers Remarks on Missile Defense. Transcript. The Federal Document Clearing House. May 1, 2001.

[29] Donald H. Rumsfeld, "Towards 21st Century Deterrence," *Wall Street Journal*, June 27, 2001.

believed that the two nations should work together to lessen or eliminate threats to their security, rather than pursue agreements based on the premise that each is a threat to the other.

Some in the Bush Administration also objected to the negotiation of new bilateral arms control agreements because the process could be too slow and too rigid. Specifically, according to one official, "formal arms control agreements that require so much time to negotiate and are negotiated at a level of detail that has become astounding... will not allow us to make the kinds of adjustments to our own forces in the timeframes we need to make them."[30] In contrast, according to Administration officials, unilateral reductions and adjustments in the U.S. force structure would allow the United States to reduce its forces quickly when they were no longer needed and restore forces quickly if conditions changed again.

President Bush announced his plans for unilateral reductions in U.S. strategic nuclear weapons in November 2001, at a press conference with Russia's President Vladimir Putin. He said that the United States would reduce its forces without signing a formal agreement with Russia because "a new relationship based upon trust and cooperation is one that doesn't need endless hours of arms control discussions.... We don't need arms control negotiations to reduce our weaponry in a significant way."[31] Although President Putin stated that he appreciated the President's decision to reduce U.S. strategic offensive weapons and noted that Russia "will try to respond in kind," he emphasized that Russia preferred to use the formal arms control process to reduce U.S. and Russian forces.[32] Russia continued to value arms control negotiations because they provided a forum to discuss sensitive security issues with the United States. According to many analysts, with its loss of territory after the collapse of the Soviet Union and its economic troubles during the 1990s, Russia saw nuclear weapon as the sole remaining measure of its superpower status.[33] Hence, arms control negotiations not only provided Russia with information about U.S. plans, programs, and policy, they also offered Russia a degree of status in international politics.

The Bush Administration eventually altered its approach and agreed to negotiate with Russia, although it preferred a less formal agreement, rather than a treaty, that would simply codify the reductions the Administration had already announced. However, reports indicate that the U.S. Senate objected to this approach. Members did not object to the possible unilateral reduction of U.S. nuclear weapons, as the Bush Administration initially preferred. However, they argued that, if the United States and Russia signed a legally binding document that obligated the United States to reduce its weapons, then the document should be a treaty, not an executive agreement. Specifically, Senators Joseph Biden and Jesse Helms pressed the Administration to submit the eventual agreement to the Senate as a treaty. They noted that "significant obligations by the United States regarding deployed U.S. strategic nuclear warheads" would "constitute a treaty subject to the advice and consent of the Senate."[34]

---

[30] "Bush Administration Reviewing Value of Arms Control Agreements.," *Inside Defense*, August 28, 2008.

[31] White House, Office of the Press Secretary. Press Conference. President Bush and President Putin Discuss New Relationship. November 13, 2001.

[32] Ibid.

[33] While some observers question whether Russia's nuclear weapons can secure its international status in light of its demographic and economic weakness, most agree that Russian officials believe and behave as they can. See Matthew Rojansky, "Russia and Strategic Stability," in *Strategic Stability: Contending Interpretations*, ed. Elbridge A. Colby and Michael S. Gerson (Carlisle, PA: Strategic Studies Institute and U.S. Army War College Press, 2013), pp. 297-299. See, also, Stephen J. Blank, *"Russia and Nuclear Weapons,"* in *Russian Nuclear Weapons: Past Present and Future,"* (Carlisle, PA: Strategic Studies Institute and U.S. Army War College Press, 2011) pp. 293-364.

[34] Thom Shanker, "Senators Insist on Role in Nuclear Arms Deals," *New York Times*, March 17, 2002, p. 16.

As a result, the George W. Bush Administration eventually agreed to codify its proposed limits in the 2002 Strategic Offensive Reductions Treaty, which became known as the Moscow Treaty. But this Treaty did not contain any detailed definitions or descriptions of the weapons to be limited, as had the START Treaty, and it did not contain any monitoring or verification provisions. During the hearings in the Senate on the Moscow Treaty, Administration officials stated that the two sides could continue to use the monitoring provisions in START to collect information about compliance with the Moscow Treaty.[35] However, START was due to expire in 2009, three years before the Moscow Treaty reductions would expire. As a result, the United States and Russia began discussions in 2006 on further arms control steps that would, at a minimum, extend the monitoring and verification provisions in START through the end of the Moscow Treaty.

In these discussions, Russia sought a formal treaty that would replace START with limits, definitions, and monitoring provisions that reached a level of detail similar to that in START. The Bush Administration, however, did not want to sign a formal treaty that would mandate further reductions in nuclear weapons. Secretary of State Condoleezza Rice argued that the current U.S.-Russian relationship did not require "the kind of highly articulated, expensive limitations and verification procedures that attended the strategic arms relationship with the Soviet Union."[36] However, as the discussions continued, the United States accepted the view that the two sides should at least extend some of the monitoring and verification provisions in START, as transparency and cooperation remained important to stability and predictability.[37] Through most of this time, the United States resisted Russia's insistence on a formal treaty, suggesting, instead, that the two sides adopt a less formal arrangement that might include voluntary notifications and site visits.[38] The United States eventually agreed to attach the monitoring provisions to a legally-binding document, although this document would have simply repeated the limits in the Moscow Treaty. The monitoring provisions would have allowed the two sides to request visits to some facilities; they would not have required the more intrusive inspections permitted under START,[39] Russia rejected the U.S. proposal, and the two sides failed to reach an agreement before the end of the Bush Administration.

Early in his first term, President Obama pledged to reduce the numbers of nuclear weapons in the U.S. arsenal by negotiating a new strategic arms reduction treaty. He stated that he and President Medvedev of Russia had agreed that they would "seek a new agreement ... that is legally binding and sufficiently bold."[40] The Administration considered these negotiations to be a part of its effort to "reset" U.S.-Russian relations. As they had during the Cold War, the negotiations might provide an area of dialogue and cooperation that could help "rebuild confidence" in the broader relationship.[41]

---

[35] U.S. Congress, Senate Foreign Relations, *Treaty on Strategic Offensive Reduction: The Moscow Treaty*, Hearing, 107th Cong., 2nd sess., July 9, 2002, S. Hrg. 107-622 (Washington: GPO, 2002), p. 6.

[36] Wade Boese. "U.S., Russia at Odds on Key Arms Issues." Arm Control Today. April 2008.

[37] U.S. State Department. Office of the Spokesman. Joint Statement by U.S. Secretary of State Condoleezza Rice and Minister for Foreign Affairs of the Russian Federation Sergey Lavrov. July 3, 2007.

[38] Nicholas Kralev. "Russia, U.S. to Discuss START." Washington Times. March 6, 2007. p. 1.

[39] Nicholas Kralev, "U.S. to Stop Counting New Missiles in Russia," Washington Times, December 1, 2009, p. 1.

[40] The White House. Office of the Press Secretary. Remarks By President Barack H. Obama, Hradcany Square Prague, Czech Republic, April 5, 2009. http://www.whitehouse.gov/the_press_office/Remarks-By-President-Barack-Obama-In-Prague-As-Delivered.

[41] See, for, example, the comments of Ambassador Rose Gottemoeller, in U.S. Department of State, *START Treaty Follow-On Talks*, Press Availability, Rome, Italy, April 24, 2009, http://www.state.gov/t/avc/rls/123065 htm.

In contrast with the position taken by the Bush Administration, the Obama Administration stated that "Russia's nuclear force will remain a significant factor in determining how much and how fast we are prepared to reduce U.S. forces." In the 2010 Nuclear Posture Review (NPR) report, the Administration indicated that "the need for strict numerical parity between the two countries is no longer as compelling as it was during the Cold War. But large disparities in nuclear capabilities could raise concerns on both sides and among U.S. allies and partners, and may not be conducive to maintaining a stable, long-term strategic relationship."[42] According to the Administration, a negotiated agreement would allow the United States and Russia "to preserve stability at significantly reduced force levels."[43] Specifically, "the verification and transparency measures included in the Treaty will help ensure stability and predictability in the U.S.-Russia strategic relationship."[44]

The United States and Russia began negotiations on a New Strategic Arms Reduction Treaty (New START) in May 2009. The goal was not only to "reset" the U.S. and Russian relationship and negotiate further reductions in the numbers of deployed strategic warheads, but also to extend the monitoring and verification provisions in the original START Treaty. The countries hoped to complete the new Treaty quickly so that it could enter into force before, or close after December 2009, when START was set to expire. However, the United States and Russia did not sign New START until April 10, 2010. After months of hearings and debate in the U.S. Senate and Russian parliament, the New START Treaty entered into force on February 5, 2011.

The Obama Administration views New START as the first step on a path to deeper reductions in the numbers of deployed strategic nuclear weapons. President Obama emphasized this point in March 2012, when he said:

> My administration's nuclear posture recognizes that the massive nuclear arsenal we inherited from the cold war is poorly suited to today's threats, including nuclear terrorism. So last summer, I directed my national security team to conduct a comprehensive study of our nuclear forces. That study is still underway. But even as we have more work to do, we can already say with confidence that we have more nuclear weapons than we need. Even after new START, the United States will still have more than 1,500 deployed nuclear weapons and some 5,000 warheads. I firmly believe that we can ensure the security of the United States and our allies, maintain a strong deterrent against any threat, and still pursue further reductions in our nuclear arsenal.[45]

The President continued his remarks by noting that the United States would seek these reductions in cooperation with Russia. He said, "Going forward, we'll continue to seek discussions with Russia on a step we have never taken before, reducing not only our strategic nuclear warheads, but also tactical weapons and warheads in reserve.... And I'm confident that, working together, we can continue to make progress and reduce our nuclear stockpiles." This goal of negotiating further reductions with Russia remains a part of U.S. arms control policy. In February 2013, Rose Gottemoeller, the Acting Under Secretary for Arms Control and International Security said, "The

---

[42] U.S. Department of Defense, *Nuclear Posture Review*, Washington, DC, April 9, 2010, p. 30, http://www.defense.gov/npr/docs/2010%20Nuclear%20Posture%20Review%20Report.pdf.

[43] Ibid., p. 19.

[44] Ibid., p. 12.

[45] President Obama, Remarks at Hankuk University of Foreign Studies in Seoul, South Korean, March 26, 2012. http://www.gpo.gov/fdsys/pkg/DCPD-201200215/pdf/DCPD-201200215.pdf.

Administration continues to believe that the next step in nuclear arms reductions should be pursued on a bilateral basis."[46]

President Obama confirmed his commitment to reduce U.S. nuclear weapons further during a speech in Berlin on June 19, 2013. He stated that he believes the United States can maintain its security, and that of its allies, with reductions of up to one-third in the number of deployed strategic nuclear warheads. He further indicated that he would seek negotiated reductions with Russia to move beyond Cold War nuclear postures. He did not, however, specify that such reductions must occur in a formal treaty, and press reports indicate that the President may prefer to seek such reductions in parallel with Russia, but without a formal treaty.[47]

The Obama Administration has also supported negotiated agreements, as opposed to unilateral measures, to address possible changes in NATO's nuclear posture. The United States currently stores around 200 nuclear bombs at NATO bases in Europe. In did not alter this posture in the 2010 Nuclear Posture Review, indicating, instead, that any changes would occur "thorough review within—and decision by—the Alliance."[48] Secretary of State Hillary Clinton addressed this issue, however, in April 2010 when she said that the removal of U.S. nuclear weapons in Europe should be linked to a reduction in the number of Russian nonstrategic nuclear weapons.[49] NATO, in its 2010 Strategic Concept, essentially endorsed this view. It indicated that it would "seek to create the conditions for further reductions" in these weapons in the future. But it indicated that "any further steps must take into account the disparity with the greater Russian stockpiles of short-range nuclear weapons."[50]

The United States and Russia have not yet started negotiations on further reductions in either strategic or nonstrategic weapons, and it is not clear that they will be able to reach a formal agreement in the near future. Nevertheless, in his speech in Berlin on June 19, 2013, the President stated that he planned to engage with U.S. allies in Europe and with Russia to develop proposals for reductions in nonstrategic nuclear weapons.[51]

Unilateral Adjustments

Nonstrategic Nuclear Weapons

As was noted above, the United States implemented significant reductions in its nonstrategic nuclear weapons as a result of the PNIs announced in September 1991, leaving it with approximately 1,100 nonstrategic nuclear weapons through the 1990s. Of this number, around

---

[46] U.S. Department of State, Office of the Undersecretary of State., *Priorities for Arms Control Negotiations Post-New START*, Remarks at the Exchange Monitor's Fifth Annual Nuclear Deterrence Summit, Arlington, VA. February 21, 2013. http://www.state.gov/t/us/205051.htm.

[47] Adam Entous and Julian E. Barnes, "U.S. to Propose New Phase In Nuclear-Arms Cuts," *Wall Street Journal*, June 19, 2013.

[48] Ibid., p. 32.

[49] "U.S. ties Removal of European Nukes to Russian Arms Cuts," Global Security Newswire, April 23, 2010.

[50] North Atlantic Treaty Organization (NATO), *Active Engagement, Modern Defense*, Strategic Concept for the Defence and Security of the Members of the North Atlantic Treaty Organization, Lisbon, Portugal, November 20, 2012, p. 24. http://www.nato.int/strategic-concept/pdf/Strat_Concept_web_en.pdf.

[51] Peter Baker and David E. Sanger, "Obama Has Plans to Cut U.S. Nuclear Arsenal, if Russia Reciprocates," *New York Times*, June 19, 2013.

---

500 were air-delivered bombs deployed at bases in Europe. The remainder, including some additional air-delivered bombs and around 320 nuclear-armed sea-launched cruise missiles, were held in storage areas in the United States.[52] The Clinton Administration altered the readiness of some of the remaining weapons, but it did not recommend or implement any further reductions in the number of U.S. nuclear weapons deployed in Europe.[53]

According to unclassified reports, the George W. Bush Administration did implement further reductions in the number of nuclear weapons deployed in Europe and the number of facilities that house those weapons, leaving the United States with fewer than 200 air-delivered B61 bombs at 5 locations. Some reports indicate that the weapons were withdrawn from Greece and Ramstein Air Base in Germany between 2001 and 2005. In addition, reports indicate that the United States withdrew its nuclear weapons from the RAF Lakenheath air base in the United Kingdom in 2006.[54] These reductions occurred without any public announcements and without any effort to negotiate reciprocal reductions with Russia. The Bush Administration also did not seek approval from Congress before implementing these changes.

As was noted above, the Obama Administration believes that the United States and NATO should seek an agreement with Russia before changing the size and structure of the U.S. force of nonstrategic nuclear weapons deployed in Europe. However, the Obama Administration did announce one unilateral adjustment to the U.S. nuclear force as a result of the 2010 Nuclear Posture Review. The Administration indicated that the Navy would retire its stockpile of nuclear-armed sea-launched cruise missiles. The George H. W. Bush Administration had removed these missiles from U.S. surface ships and attack submarines as a part of the 1991 PNIs. The Clinton Administration and George W. Bush Administration had retained these missiles, and the capability to restore them to submarines, as a part of the U.S. effort to assure its allies in Asia of the U.S. commitment to their defense. However, the missiles have aged, and the Navy had no plans to replace them. The Obama Administration decided to retire them and to rely on other U.S. nuclear capabilities to assure U.S. allies in Asia.

Nondeployed Weapons

As was noted above, the U.S. stockpile of nondeployed nuclear weapons stood at almost 14,000 warheads in 1992. The stockpile continued to decline early in the Clinton Administration, as the United States completed the adjustments that were associated with the 1991 PNIs and the Bush-era changes in U.S. nuclear strategy. By 1994, the number of warheads in the stockpile had declined to about 11,000, a reduction of around 50% from the stockpile that had existed at the beginning of the George H.W. Bush Administration. The Clinton Administration did not authorize any significant further reductions however, and the stockpile remained at about 10,600 nondeployed warheads in 2000.

---

[52] Hans M. Kristensen and Robert S. Norris, "NRDC Nuclear Notebook: U.S. Nuclear Forces, 2007," *Bulletin of the Atomic Scientists*, January/February 2007.

[53] Under the 1991 PNIs, the Navy removed all nonstrategic nuclear weapons from surface ships and attack submarines, but it retained the capability, with appropriate training and resources, to redeploy these weapons if conditions changed. The Clinton Administration eliminated this capability for surface ships, but retained the Navy's ability to restore nuclear-armed cruise missiles to attack submarines.

[54] Hans M. Kristensen, U.S. Nuclear Weapons Withdrawn from the United Kingdom. Federation of American Scientists, Strategic Security Blog. June 26, 2008, http://www.fas.org/blog/ssp/2008/06/us-nuclear-weapons-withdrawn-from-the-united-kingdom.php.

The George W. Bush Administration resumed reductions in the U.S. nuclear stockpile, indicating that it planned to reduce the U.S. nuclear stockpile by between 50% and 60%, although it never released the actual numbers of warheads in the stockpile or the number affected by the reductions. When the Obama Administration released an unclassified summary of the size of the U.S. stockpile in May 2010, it showed that the United States had a stockpile of 5,113 deployed, nondeployed, and inactive warheads in 2009, a decline of nearly 60% from the stockpile of 2000.[55] These reductions reflect changes, identified and adopted after the 2001 Nuclear Posture Review, in assessments of the number of warheads needed to meet U.S. national security. The Bush Administration implemented these reductions without seeking or expecting reciprocity from Russia. Congress had the opportunity to review the Administration's plans for the nuclear stockpile during the annual authorization and appropriations process. It did not object to the planned reductions, although it did seek to restrain programs that the Bush Administration sought to fund to design and develop new types of nuclear warheads.[56]

During its first term, the Obama Administration continued to reduce the size of the U.S. nuclear stockpile, although at a much slower pace than that achieved during the Bush Administration. Recent reports indicate that the stockpile has declined by around 500 warheads since 2009, reaching a level of around 4,650 warheads in early 2014.[57] This reduction likely occured as a result of the retirement of the nuclear-armed sea-launched cruise missiles.

Role of Congress in the Arms Control Process

If the Obama Administration pursues additional reductions in U.S. nuclear weapons, Congress will have an opportunity to influence implementation.[58] The path for this influence depends, in part, on the mechanism the Administration uses to reduce U.S. nuclear forces. If they sign a formal, legally-binding agreement that mandates reductions in nuclear forces, the President would likely submit it to the Senate as a new treaty or as an amendment to New START. As an alternative, the United States and Russia could incorporate legally-binding limits in an Executive Agreement. If the United States and Russia cannot, or choose not to, agree on formal, legally-binding reductions, the President could simply state his intent to reduce U.S. nuclear weapons, either verbally or in writing, in parallel with a similar commitment from Russia. He could also arguably state his intent to reduce the size and structure of the U.S. arsenal unilaterally, without reciprocity from Russia, as long as Congress appropriated the necessary funds to implement the reductions.

---

[55] U.S. Department of Defense. Fact Sheet. Increasing Transparency in the U.S. Nuclear Weapons Stockpile. May 3, 2010. http://www.defense.gov/npr/docs/10-05-03_fact_sheet_us_nuclear_transparency__final_w_date.pdf.

[56] See, for example, CRS Report RL33748, *Nuclear Warheads: The Reliable Replacement Warhead Program and the Life Extension Program*, by Jonathan E. Medalia, and CRS Report RL32130, *Nuclear Weapon Initiatives: Low-Yield R&D, Advanced Concepts, Earth Penetrators, Test Readiness*, by Jonathan E. Medalia.

[57] Hans M. Kristensen and Robert S. Norris, "U.S. Nuclaer Forces, 2014," *Bulletin of the Atomic Scientists*, vol. 70, no. 1 (January 2014). http://bos.sagepub.com/content/70/1/85 full.pdf+html.

[58] Congress can also play a role during the negotiation of arms control agreements. For a detailed review of the Congressional role in arms control, see U.S. Congress, House Committee on Foreign Affairs, Subcommittee on Arms Control, International Security and Science, *Fundamentals of Nuclear Arms Control: Part IX, The Congressional Role in Nuclear Arms*, committee print, prepared by the Congressional Research Service, 99th Cong., 2nd sess., June 1986 (Washington: GPO, 1986). http://rsinquery.loc.gov/crsx/products-nd/86.1350.doc.pdf.

Legally-Binding Treaty or Executive Agreement

If the United States and Russia sign a new arms control treaty, the President would have to submit it to the Senate for its advice and consent to ratification. Specifically, the U.S. Constitution states that the President "shall have the power, by and with the Advice and Consent of the Senate, to make Treaties, provided two-thirds of the Senators present concur."[59] Senate committees would hold hearings, craft a resolution of ratification, and vote on that resolution. The resolution would require a two-thirds majority to pass.[60]

If the United States and Russia were to alter New START with changes that imposed a legally-binding obligation on the United States, it seems likely that the President would need to submit these proposed amendments to the Senate for its advice and consent. The Senate emphasized this point in Declaration 9 of the Resolution of Ratification to New START, when it stated "that any agreement or understanding which in any material way modifies, amends, or reinterprets United States or Russian obligations under the New START Treaty, including the time frame for implementation of the New START Treaty, should be submitted to the Senate for its advice and consent to ratification."[61]

Although the United States has historically entered into most major arms control agreements by way of treaty, such agreements could take another form and still be legally binding and constitutionally valid.[62] A congressional-executive agreement would not require the advice and consent of the Senate in order to enter force for the United States. Instead, the agreement would be authorized by means of a statute approved by both houses of Congress.[63] The United States used this mechanism to codify limits on offensive forces in1972, as a part of the Strategic Arms Limitation Talks (SALT).

The requirement that the President seek congressional approval if he reduces U.S. nuclear forces through an agreement with another nation appears in the Arms Control and Disarmament Act of 1961. This legislation, as amended in 1994, states that "No action shall be taken pursuant to this

---

[59] U.S. Const. Article II, Section 2. For further background, see United States Senate, Committee on Foreign Relations. Treaties and Other International Agreements: The Role of the United States Senate. Committee print, prepared by the Congressional Research Service. p. 2.

[60] For a description of the process in which the Senate considers treaties, see CRS Report 98-384, *Senate Consideration of Treaties*, by Valerie Heitshusen. A table detailing the treaty ratification process can be found at CRS Report RL32528, *International Law and Agreements: Their Effect upon U.S. Law*, by Michael John Garcia, p. 15.

[61] U.S. Congress, Senate Committee on Foreign Relations, *Treaty with Russia on Further Reduction and Limitation of Strategic Offensive Arms (The New START Treaty)*, Executive Report, 111th Cong., 2nd sess., October 1, 2010, Exec.Rept. 111-6 (Washington: GPO, 2010), p. 9.

[62] For a more detailed explanation of the differences between treaties and executive agreements, see CRS Report RL32528, *International Law and Agreements: Their Effect upon U.S. Law*, by Michael John Garcia. Analysis of the potential constitutional impediments to the entering and enforcement of such agreements by the Executive are beyond the scope of this report.

[63] U.S. Congress, Senate Committee on Foreign Relations, *Treaties and Other International Agreements: The Role of the United States Senate*, committee print, prepared by the Congressional Research Service, 103rd Cong., 1st sess., November 1993, S. Prt. 103-53 (Washington: GPO, 1993), p. 54. Not every executive agreement must be approved via legislation. Executive agreements implementing a requirement of a ratified treaty, or that are entered pursuant to the President's independent constitutional authority, are also occasionally made by the United States. Even assuming that either form of executive agreement would be a constitutionally valid means for entering an arms reduction agreement, the Arms Control and Disarmament Act of 1961, as amended, would appear to limit the legal effect of such an agreement. 22 USC Section 2573 (generally requiring arms reduction agreements to take the form of treaties or be authorized by statutory enactment).

chapter or any other Act that would obligate the United States to reduce or limit the Armed Forces or armaments of the United States in a militarily significant manner, except pursuant to the treaty-making power of the President set forth in Article II, Section 2, clause 2 of the Constitution or unless authorized by the enactment of further affirmative legislation by the Congress of the United States."[64]

While the 1961 Act remains controlling law, the Senate indicated in a declaration to the New START Resolution of Ratification that it would seek to ensure that any arms reduction agreement take the form of a treaty presented to the Senate for its advice and consent.[65] Specifically, the Senate narrowed this requirement a bit in Declaration 11B of the New START Resolution of Ratification when it stated that "the Senate declares that further arms reduction agreements obligating the United States to reduce or limit the Armed Forces or armaments of the United States in any militarily significant manner be made only pursuant to the treaty-making power of the President as set forth in Article II, Section 2, clause 2 of the Constitution of the United States." In other words, the Senate expects any future arms control agreement to come to the Senate as a treaty, not to the whole of Congress as a congressional-executive agreement.

Non-legal, Political Agreement

The 1961 Arms Control and Reduction Act generally bars the Executive from taking action that would "obligate" the United States to reduce armaments in a military significant manner unless such action takes the form of a treaty or is affirmatively authorized by Congress. It might be argued that the word "obligate" refers to the imposition of the legal duty upon the United States to reduce its armaments, and would not bar the Executive from reducing U.S. nuclear forces either unilaterally or in parallel with Russia on the basis of a nonlegal political agreement between the two countries. On occasion, the United States has made nonlegal political commitments or "gentlemen's agreements" with other countries. Such agreements are understood to have no legal effect, though they may carry significant political or moral weight.[66]

Under the executive branch interpretation of ACDA, a document that contained a political, but not legally-binding, commitment would not require the advice and consent of the Senate or an affirmative vote of both the House and Senate. The document could make its intent clear with a distinct statement indicating that it was only politically binding, or that it did not require the two nations to assume new legal obligations. Even if it did not include a specific statement, the agreement could make it clear with other language that each side was simply declaring its own intentions and recording those intentions in a joint statement. For example, they could state that they *intended* to reduce their forces even though they were not *obligated* to do so.

---

[64] 22 USC Section 2573.

[65] Declarations made by the Senate when approving a treaty are generally not viewed as establishing enforceable U.S. law themselves, but instead constitute "statements expressing the Senate's position or opinion on matters relating to issues raised by the treaty rather than to specific provisions." .S. Congress, Senate Committee on Foreign Relations, *Treaties and Other International Agreements: The Role of the United States Senate*, committee print, prepared by the Congressional Research Service, 103rd Cong., 1st sess., November 1993, S. Prt. 103-53 (Washington: GPO, 1993), p. 11.

[66] The State Department has published guidance regarding the format that a non-legally binding agreement should take. U.S. Department of State, Office of the Legal Adviser, Guidance on Non-Binding Documents. http://www.state.gov/s/l/treaty/guidance/.

Numerous Administrations have claimed that the President has the authority to reach such agreements without congressional authorization, though such commitments have on occasion sparked significant controversy and occasional legislative opposition.[67] In any event because a political commitment does not have the force of law, the President's ability to implement the commitment would be limited by preexisting legal constraints, whether constitutional or statutory in nature, or by funding restrictions adopted by Congress.[68]

The United States and Russia have concluded politically binding statements within the framework of previous arms control agreements. For example, when they signed the 1991 START Treaty, they agreed to exchange declarations on nuclear-armed sea-launched cruise missiles (SLCMs). The Soviet Union wanted to count these missiles under the Treaty limits because it believed the United States could use them to attack strategic targets on Soviet territory. The United States rejected this effort because the limits might capture both nuclear-armed and conventionally-armed SLCMs, as it was extremely difficult to verify the type of warhead on the missile. As a result, SLCMs did not count under the Treaty limits, but the United States and Soviet Union issued unilateral, but identical, statements about them. They each declared that they would exchange annual declarations specifying the maximum number of deployed nuclear SLCMs planned each of the following five years. They also indicated that the number of deployed nuclear SLCMs declared during the term of the Treaty would not exceed 880 in any one year.[69] To ensure that this number did not represent a legally-binding limit on the number of deployed SLCMs, both the U.S. and Russian statements stated that "This declaration and subsequent annual declarations will be politically binding." As was noted earlier, the United States withdrew all of its nuclear-armed SLCMs from deployment under the 1991 PNIs. Nevertheless, the nations exchanged these annual declarations while START remained in force.

Authorization and Appropriations

If the Obama Administration sought to reduce U.S. nuclear weapons unilaterally, or in parallel with Russia without a legally-binding agreement, Congress could still exercise oversight of the process. It could, for example, pass legislation expressing the sense of Congress about the process that the United States should pursue in seeking further reductions. For example, the National Defense Authorization Act for 2014 states, "It is the sense of Congress that, if the United States seeks further strategic nuclear arms reductions with the Russian Federation that are below the levels of the New START Treaty" such reductions should be pursued through a negotiated agreement and "be made pursuant to the treaty-making power of the President."[70]

Congress could also used funding decisions to influence the arms control process. For example, in 1968 and 1969, Congress tried, unsuccessfully, to reduce funding for the emerging U.S. Sentinel

---

[67] U.S. Library of Congress, Congressional Research Service, "Gentlemen's Agreements" with Foreign Entities: Congressional Oversight. Legal Side Bar. August 8, 2012. http://www.crs.gov/analysis/legalsidebar/pages/details.aspx?ProdId=14.

[68] U.S. Library of Congress, Congressional Research Service, "Gentlemen's Agreements" with Foreign Entities: Congressional Oversight. Legal Side Bar. August 8, 2012. http://www.crs.gov/analysis/legalsidebar/pages/details.aspx?ProdId=14.

[69] U.S. Department of State, Bureau of Arms Control, Verification, and Compliance, The Treaty Between the United States of America and the Union of Soviet Socialist Republics on the Reduction and Limitation of Strategic Offensive Arms (START), Associated Documents, July 31, 1991, http://www.state.gov/documents/organization/27390.pdf.

[70] H.R. 3304, Sec. 1060.

and Safeguard anti-ballistic missile (ABM) systems.[71] These efforts failed, but the votes narrowed each year. In 1969, the Senate approved the first phase of development, but only after Vice President Spiro Agnew cast a tie-breaking vote. In 1970, amendments that would restrict funding to the deployment of only two Safeguard sites again failed. But, in1972, the United States and Soviet Union signed the ABM Treaty, which restricted each side to two sites for its ABM systems. Hence, after Congress, through its votes on funding for the system, demonstrated its growing support for restraint in the deployment of the ABM system, the Nixon Administration agreed to exercise such restraint.

Congress also sought to influence the arms control process with funding restrictions in the latter half of the1990s. During the 1994 Nuclear Posture Review, the Defense Department had decided that it would retire all 50 Peacekeeper ICBMs and four if its eighteen Ohio-class ballistic missile submarines to meet the START II limits. These decisions were incorporated in DOD's budget plans, even though START II had not entered into force. To prevent the early retirement of these systems, Congress stated, in the 1997 Defense Authorization Act, that "funds available to the Department of Defense may not be obligated or expended during fiscal year 1997 for retiring or dismantling, or for preparing to retire or dismantle" any of the bombers, missiles, or submarines limited by the START II Treaty.[72] The funding limitation could be waived if START II entered into force, but, even in that case, funding could not be used "to implement any agreement or understanding to undertake substantial early deactivation" of these systems until "30 days after the date on which the President submits to Congress a report concerning such actions." In other words, the legislation recognized that the President could reach a politically-binding agreement with Russia to accelerate the implementation of the Treaty, but, if he did, he would have to report to Congress about the agreement before he could implement it.[73]

Initially, Congress passed this funding limitation to provide the Russian parliament with an incentive to approve the START II Treaty—it clearly stated that U.S. forces would not decline further until START II entered into force. The Clinton Administration sought to ease the restriction in subsequent years as the budgetary cost to retain aging systems increased. However, because many in Congress opposed the Clinton Administration's nuclear weapons policies, Congress included similar provisions in the Defense Authorization Bills for FY1999, FY2000, and FY2001. It did, however, repeal this language for the Bush Administration in the FY2002 Defense Bill, after the 2001 Nuclear Posture Review called for the elimination of the Peacekeeper missiles and the conversion of the four Ohio-class submarines.

Some in Congress have sought to incorporate similar funding limitations on the reduction of U.S. nuclear forces in recent versions of the National Defense Authorization Act. For example, Section 1055 the House version of the Defense Authorization Act for 2012 (H.R. 1540) stated that the

---

[71] U.S. Congress, House Committee on Foreign Affairs, Subcommittee on Arms Control, International Security and Science, *Fundamentals of Nuclear Arms Control. Part IX, The Congressional Role in Nuclear Arms*, committee print, prepared by The Congressional Research Service, 99th Cong., 2nd sess., June 1986 (Washington: GPO, 1986), pp. 12-13.

[72] P.L. 104-201, Section 1302.

[73] The language in the 1997 Defense Authorization Act applied the funding limitation to the deactivation of all U.S. strategic delivery systems, even those that would have been retired under the original START Treaty. As a result, in the 1998 legislation, Congress altered the language to indicate that the limitation applied only to those systems that would have remained under START I but were to be retired under START II. See U .S. Congress. National Defense Authorization Act for Fiscal Year 1998. Conference Report to accompany H.R. 1119. (H.Rept. 105-340, Section 1302.) October 23, 1997. p. 332.

Secretary of Defense and the Secretary of Energy could not fund programs to retire any systems covered by New START, unless they could issue a positive report on the status plans to maintain and modernize the U.S. nuclear enterprise. The prohibition applied not only to the delivery systems, but also to the warheads or gravity bombs that could be delivered by these systems. New START does not require the elimination of any warheads or gravity bombs, although the United States eliminates some number of these each year as it manages the drawdown of the U.S. stockpile.

The legislation in the late 1990s sought to limit the President's ability to reduce nuclear weapons below legally-binding treaty obligations; those in the 2012 legislation sought to prevent the President from complying with the New START Treaty's limits. This legislation could have produced a legal quandary if it required that the President violate the terms of the Treaty. The Conference Committee modified the language and the final version of the act (P.L. 112-81, Section 1045) states that the United States should provide the necessary resources to maintain a "safe, secure, reliable, and credible nuclear deterrent." If the resources fall short of those anticipated at the time of New START's ratification, then the President should submit a report detailing the shortfall's effects and a plan to address them. The legislation did not withhold funding for the implementation of New START pending the completion of that report or a restoration of lost funding.

Congress has also, recently, sought to prevent the President from reducing U.S. nuclear forces below the limits in New START. Specifically, the House version of the NDAA for 2014 (H.R. 1960), stated, "None of the funds authorized to be appropriated by this Act or otherwise made available for fiscal year 2014" could be used to "retire, dismantle, or deactivate, or prepare to retire, dismantle, or deactivate" any delivery vehicle covered by the New START Treaty if it would reduce the size of the U.S. force below the New START limit of 800. According to the legislation, the Presient could waive this limitation only if the Senate had given its advice and consent to a new treaty and that treaty had entered into force. Congress did not include this language in the final version of the NDAA for 2014 (H.R. 3304), but, as noted above, it did express its view that further reductions should occur through the treaty process.

Characteristics Affecting Arms Control Decisions

The preceding discussion highlights several characteristics—balance and equality, predictability, flexibility, transparency and confidence in compliance, and timeliness—that can affect a decision to use a formal, bilateral treaty, informal parallel reductions, or unilateral adjustments to alter the size or structure of the U.S. nuclear arsenal. Some of these characteristics may weigh more heavily than others at different times, reflecting conditions in the international security environment and domestic political environment. This section describes each of these characteristics in more detail. It includes examples from numerous arms control endeavors that highlight the presence or absence of concern for the characteristics and the way in which this concern promoted a unilateral, bilateral, or, perhaps, mixed approach to reduce U.S. nuclear forces. Additional details about these arms control endeavors can be found in CRS Report RL33865, *Arms Control and Nonproliferation: A Catalog of Treaties and Agreements.*

Balance and Equality

When negotiating formal treaties during the Cold War, the United States and Soviet Union sought provisions that appeared balanced and equal, in spite of differences in their weapon systems and force structures. In seeking this balance, each nation acknowledged that the size and structure of its forces could affect the other nation's assessment of its security. In addition, the process allowed the parties to interact as equals—with an equal sense of security and an equal sense of sacrifice—in a way that appeared to enhance understanding and stability. Nevertheless, the need to determine balanced trades between different types of weapons systems often added months or years to the negotiating process.

Analysts have debated, over the years, about whether balance and equality contribute to stability and reduce the risk of nuclear war.[74] Many support the idea that a measure of equality and a sense of balance can reduce arms race incentives, where the nations might seek to acquire more weapons or new types of weapons to offset apparent disadvantages or expand potential advantages. Such an arms race could lead to instabilities if a nation believed it had suddenly become vulnerable to a first strike or if it believed it may have a short window of advantage when it might achieve a successful first strike. Others, however, support the idea that, in seeking a measure of balance and equality, arms control agreements can lock nations into force structures that might become destabilizing over time, particularly if new technologies or new threats emerge outside the framework of the arms control treaty.[75] Under these circumstances, the existence of a formal, bilateral treaty might actually increase instability and increase the risk of war.

These alternative views have been evident in U.S. arms control policy over the years. In the early1970s, the United States signed an Interim Agreement on Offensive Arms that capped the number of missiles in both sides' forces, but because the forces were of different sizes, the limits on each were not equal. Congress objected to this outcome and mandated that all future treaties with the Soviet Union include equal limits on both sides. Subsequent treaties with the Soviet Union and Russia have included equal limits, at least in the aggregate, and sometimes have included equal sublimits on different categories of weapons. Some treaties have specified a single agreed limit for both sides, while others have referred to an agreed range for the aggregate limit—for example, the parties could deploy between 3,000 and 3,500 warheads under START II and between1,700 and 2,200 warheads under the Moscow Treaty—to accommodate different force structure plans. But, even though each side would have likely chosen force level within the range, the range applied equally to both.

---

[74] "Stability" is a term with several possible definitions and applications. In this report, it usually refers to the sense that neither the United States nor Soviet Union/Russia would have an incentive to launch a first strike with nuclear weapons, both because its forces could survive and retaliate after absorbing an attack and because it lacked the ability to deny its opponent the ability to survive and retaliate after an attack. This concept of "first strike stability" has been enshrined as a goal of arms control in joint U.S.-Soviet and U.S.-Russian statements, and in the text of several arms control agreements. For example, in a Joint Statement signed during the original START negotiations in 1990, Presidents Bush and Gorbachev agreed that the reductions in START "will be designed to make a first strike less plausible. The result will be greater stability and a lower risk of war." See "Summit in Washington; Text of the Statement On Long-Range Arms," *New York Times*, June 2, 1990. http://www nytimes.com/1990/06/02/world/summit-in-washington-text-of-the-statement-on-long-range-arms.html?pagewanted=all&src=pm.

[75] For a discussion of this type of "arms control trap," see Christopher A. Ford, "Anything but Simple: Arms Control and Strategic Stability," in *Strategic Stability: Contending Interpretations*, ed. Elbridge A. Colby and Michael S. Gerson (Carlisle, PA: Strategic Studies Institute and U.S. Army War College Press, 2013), pp. 217-220.

During the 1990s, the United States and Russia continued to negotiate formal arms control treaties that sought equal limits on their deployed strategic offensive nuclear forces. Although the risk of nuclear war had receded with the end of the Cold War, this process continued to provide each nation with knowledge about the other side's nuclear capabilities. Moreover, the value placed on balanced and equal limits served as a symbol of "political balance" in the relationship between the two nations. For example, the implementation of the 1991 START Treaty and negotiation of the 1993 START II Treaty provided Russia with a sense of "equal status" and helped manage the U.S.-Russian relationship in the decade after the collapse of the Soviet Union.

As was noted above, President George H.W. Bush in 1991 and President George W. Bush in 2001 both supported unilateral reductions in U.S. nuclear forces, without seeking reciprocal reductions from the Soviet Union or Russia. In both cases, U.S. officials had decided that the United States could maintain, or even strengthen, its security without maintaining a degree of balance or equality in nuclear forces. For example, in 1991, after the collapse of the Warsaw Pact, the United States decided that it no longer needed to deploy ground-based nuclear weapons in Europe to deter or respond to an attack. The threat the weapons were to deter—Soviet and Warsaw Pact attacks in Europe—had diminished sharply. Further, the military utility of these weapons had declined as the Soviet Union pulled its forces eastward, beyond the range of these weapons, and as the United States altered its warfighting concepts at sea. The perceived absence of a need for balance and equality allowed the United States to make sweeping changes in its nuclear posture in a relatively short amount of time. This result may not have been possible if the United States had waited for the Soviet Union to agree to similar reductions.

In 2001, the George W. Bush announced that the United States would reduce its deployed strategic nuclear forces, without regard for the size or structure of Russia's nuclear force, because the Cold War was over and the U.S. relationship with Russia had improved. President Bush suggested that each nation simply declare its own preferred force size, then reduce to that level. This proposal reflected the view that it was no longer important to maintain equality across forces to ensure stability or reduce the risk of war. In addition, if the United States was not bound by the limits of a formal treaty, it could adjust its forces again, even if it needed to increase the numbers, to address emerging threats from other nations.

In 2009, the Obama Administration argued that a measure of balance and equality was important for stability, both for the nuclear balance and for the broader U.S.-Russian relationship. As was noted above, the NPR indicated, that although exact parity was not necessary, "large disparities in nuclear capabilities" could undermine "a stable, long-term strategic relationship" between the United States and Russia.[76] Thus the Administration supported negotiations on reductions in strategic nuclear weapons and nonstrategic nuclear weapons so that the two sides could avoid significant differences in the size of their forces.

However, it may not always be possible for the United States and Russia to negotiate a treaty that provides for balanced or equal reductions. The Obama Administration has indicated that it would like the next U.S.-Russian nuclear arms control treaty to cover deployed strategic nuclear weapons, nonstrategic nuclear weapons, and nondeployed nuclear weapons, possibly limiting them within an aggregate limit on all categories of warheads.[77] This formula seems to indicate

---

[76] U.S. Department of Defense, *Nuclear Posture Review*, Washington, DC, April 9, 2010, p. 30. http://www.defense.gov/npr/docs/2010%20Nuclear%20Posture%20Review%20Report.pdf.

[77] See, for example, Rose Gottemoeller, *The Obama Administration's Second Term Priorities for Arms Control and Nonproliferation*, U.S. Department of State, Remarks, Geneva, Switzerland, March 20, 2013, http://www.state.gov/t/us/ (continued...)

that balance can be achieved across the three categories of weapons, even if the two sides are not limited to equal numbers within each category. Russia, in contrast, has expressed little interest in further reductions in deployed strategic nuclear weapons and no interest in limits or reductions in nonstrategic nuclear weapons, at least until the United States withdraws all of its nonstrategic nuclear weapons from Europe.[78] Instead, Russia would like to negotiate an agreement that would limit U.S. ballistic missile defense programs, and the government argues that any further limits on strategic offensive forces must count long-range conventional, as well as nuclear weapons. Given these articulated priorities, the search for balance and equality may slow or stall the negotiations and complicate the search for a bilateral treaty.

Predictability

Formal arms control negotiations and the resulting treaties can improve each nation's ability to understand the other's forces and capabilities and allow both nations to predict how those forces might change in the future. During negotiations, the nations may share details about existing forces and insights into plans for the future so that each can understand how threats may emerge and evolve. The limits in an agreement can also provide each nation with confidence about the future size and capabilities of the other nation's forces. This knowledge, when combined with the limits in the treaty, can dampen pressures to acquire not only greater numbers of total weapons but also specific types of weapons that the nations may believe they need to overcome future, potential threats. A treaty's monitoring provisions and detailed restrictions can also provide the parties with confidence that they will not be surprised by actions taken by the other nation and that they will have sufficient warning if the other nation seeks to evade treaty-imposed limits.

The level of detail, and, therefore, the amount of predictability, included in arms control treaties grew during the 1970s and 1980s, culminating in the 1991 START Treaty. The full text of the documents associated with START fills 290 pages. This includes annexes, protocols, and associated agreements that add details to the requirements contained in the basic treaty. For example, the Definitions Annex includes 124 detailed definitions of the weapons systems, facilities, procedures, and other terms in the Treaty while the Conversion and Elimination Protocol outlines the precise procedures that the countries must follow so that weapons will no longer count under the Treaty. In contrast, the United States and Russia never codified the reductions outlined in the 1991 PNIs in a formal treaty, or in any other bilateral document. Each side simply announced the reductions in presidential speeches. As a result, they did not provide each other details about the numbers of weapons present prior to the reductions, the types of weapons included in the measures, or the actions taken to deactivate and dismantle those weapons. They have also shared little information about the number of weapons eliminated and the number of weapons remaining outside the scope of the measures. This absence of detail not only leads to occasional disputes about whether Russia has complied with its PNI obligations, but also makes it very difficult for either side to predict the future size or structure of the other's nonstrategic nuclear forces.

Predictability between the United States and Russia may be far less important today than it was during the Cold War. Both force levels and the risk of war are far lower than they were at that

---

(...continued)

206454 htm.

[78] Vladimir Kozin, "Time for TART," *The Moscow Times*, February 2010.

time so the United States and Russia may not feel threatened by changes in the size or structure of the other's nuclear force. Some experts argue that, "there is no conceivable situation in the contemporary world in which it would be in either country's national security interest to initiate a nuclear attack against the other side."[79] As a result, if each structures its forces in a way that ensures a second-strike retaliatory capability, then neither may fear the size or structure of the other side's forces. In addition, the United States and Russia cooperate across many policy areas and maintain many channels for communication; they share information about their nuclear force structure plans and raise concerns about possible future developments even in the absence of a treaty that mandated predictable force levels.

Flexibility

Flexibility is, in many ways, the opposite of equality and predictability. When an arms control treaty includes equal limits on each side's forces, so that both can confidently predict the current size and future plans for the other's force, both sides have limited flexibility to increase their forces or alter their composition to respond to technological changes or emerging national security needs. On the other hand, unilateral U.S. nuclear reductions allow the United States to set the size and structure of its nuclear force. The United States would eliminate only those weapons that it believed were no longer needed for its security and leave open the possibility of deploying greater numbers of existing weapons or new types of weapons if conditions were to change.

The United States took advantage of this flexibility when it reduced its nonstrategic forces unilaterally in 1991. When President George H.W. Bush announced the PNIs, he indicated that the United States would retain some types of weapons, including the sea-based Tomahawk cruise missiles, in storage. The Defense Department supported this approach because the weapons could be returned to deployment if the need arose.[80] Similar considerations contributed to the George W. Bush Administration's preference in 2001 for unilateral reductions in U.S. strategic nuclear forces. Press reports indicate that, although the United States eventually agreed to codify the proposed force levels in the Moscow Treaty, Pentagon officials had strongly resisted negotiations. They wanted the United States to be able to reduce or increase its nuclear forces in response to changes in the international security environment.[81]

Unilateral reductions also provide the United States with flexibility in the timing of its reductions. In 1991, the United States implemented the reductions quickly, removing bombers from alert in a matter of days and nonstrategic weapons from deployment in a matter of months. Reductions could also occur more slowly to allow for renewed consideration of security needs or to coincide with the normal retirement schedule for a weapons system. Or, as has been the case with reductions in nondeployed nuclear weapons, they can occur when the United States identifies excess weapons and has the capacity to dismantle them. Treaties, on the other hand, often set an

---

[79] Gen. (Ret.) James Cartwright et al., *Modernizing U.S. Nuclear Strategy,*, Global Zero, Global Zero U.S. Nuclear Policy Commission Report, Washington, DC, May 2012, p. 2, http://www.globalzero.org/files/gz_us_nuclear_policy_commission_report.pdf.

[80] Susan J. Koch, *Ther Presidential Nuclear Initiatives of 1991-1992*, Center for the Study of Weapons of Mass Destruction, National Defense University, Case Study Series, Washington, DC, September 2012, p. 8. http://www.ndu.edu/press/lib/pdf/CSWMD-CaseStudy/CSWMD_CaseStudy-5.pdf.

[81] Jonathan Landay. "Rumsfeld Reportedly Resists Firm Limits on Nuclear Arms," San Jose Mercury News. April 27, 2002.

arbitrary time line for weapons eliminations, which can add to the costs and increase the complexity of the process.

On the other hand, if nations reduce their forces unilaterally, even if they do so in parallel, they could eventually undermine stability. If either party, fearing that the other was about to add to its forces, sought to reverse its reductions quickly, the other might feel insecure or threatened. Further, if both lack clear information about the other's forces, the balance between the two could be unstable, resulting in a "rearmament race" or escalation of a crisis.

The 2002 Moscow Treaty and the 2010 New START Treaty both sought to combine the characteristics of predictability and flexibility. For example, although the Moscow Treaty contained an equal limit on the total number of U.S. and Russian deployed warheads, it contained no sublimits on specific systems or timetable for force reductions. Each side could structure its forces the way it wanted and reduce them at its own pace. Further, without any definitions describing the forces limited by the treaty or establishing rules for counting them, and without any requirements for data exchanges during implementation, each side simply chose its own method of counting and could declare, at the end of the treaty's implementation period, its total number of remaining forces. Then, because the treaty's implementation period concluded on December 31, 2012 and the treaty also expired at that time, either side could increase its forces immediately after it concluded the reductions.

The New START Treaty retains some of these flexible provisions. It contains an aggregate limit on the total number of deployed warheads and delivery vehicles, but it does not impose sublimits on particular systems. During the debate over the treaty, Obama Administration officials highlighted this format because it would provide the United States with the ability to structure its remaining forces to meet its own security needs.[82] And, although the treaty does contain definitions of limited systems, it does not contain specific counting rules that attribute a number of warheads to each type of delivery system. As was the case with the Moscow Treaty, each side simply declares its aggregate number of warheads. At the same time, New START retains many of the monitoring provisions from the 1991 START Treaty, so the two sides exchange substantial amounts of data about the numbers, locations, and characteristics of their deployed delivery vehicles, and they update this data regularly. They also conduct up to 18 inspections each year to confirm this data. Hence, although each side has the flexibility to structure its forces itself, the data and inspections provide a degree of transparency and predictability about those forces.

It may also be possible to balance flexibility and predictability in unilateral reductions. Even absent a formal treaty mandating reductions in their nuclear forces, the United States and Russia could exchange reciprocal statements about their intentions. They could also exchange data—periodically—and possibly permit visits or inspections, so that they could confirm, and continue to predict, the status of the other side's forces. This is similar to the type of regime the George W. Bush Administration proposed in 2008 to replace START. Russia rejected the proposal, and indicated that, under Russian law, it could not permit data exchanges and inspections unless they were part of a legally binding agreement.[83] Nevertheless, if both sides support further reductions, but each prefers to maintain a greater degree of flexibility, an informal transparency regime, or

---

[82] See, for example, the testimony of Hon. Rose Gottemoeller in U.S. Congress, Senate Foreign Relations, *The New START Treaty*, Hearing, 111th Cong., 2nd sess., June 15, 2010, S. Hrg. 111-738 (Washington: GPO, 2010), pp. 217-218.

[83] Wade Boese. "U.S., Russia exploring post-START Options." *Arms Control Today*. May 2007.

even a formal treaty that focuses on transparency and confidence-building measures, may be sufficient to provide a measure of predictability.

Transparency and Confidence in Compliance

The arms control process has played a key role in providing the participating nations with access to and an understanding of the military forces and activities of the other party. They needed this information to verify compliance with the limits and restrictions in the treaty. During the 1970s, the United States and Soviet Union relied almost exclusively on their own national technical means (NTM) to monitor forces and activities limited by arms control agreements. These included the satellites and remote sensing technologies that each nation employed to monitor the other, regardless of arms control obligations. Beginning in 1987, with the Intermediate-range Nuclear Forces (INF) Treaty, the parties also added extensive data exchanges, notifications, and on-site inspections to their mechanisms for monitoring forces and verifying compliance with arms control treaties. Many viewed these measures as a way to build trust, foster cooperation, and confirm information already collected by NTM.

Sharing data, allowing inspections, and cooperating in providing access to information are now familiar characteristics of the arms control process.[84] These activities have helped build a legacy of confidence in compliance with the treaties. The United States and Russia began adding cooperative monitoring mechanisms to arms control treaties in the late 1980s. During the negotiations, many analysts expected these measures would help the United States "catch" Soviet cheating. But, because each nation provided a wealth of data to the other and each could confirm that data with on-site access to weapons and facilities, both found that the process increased confidence in compliance. The inspections provided a ground truth that had not been present in earlier treaties and fostered cooperation between the two sides' military establishments.

There are a number of different ways that nations could approach the issue of transparency when pursuing arms control endeavors. Although it is common to associate transparency measures with the monitoring and verification regime in a formal arms control treaty, it is possible to conclude treaties that lack monitoring and verification provisions—this was the case with the 2002 Moscow Treaty and the 1972 Biological Weapons Convention—although, in some cases they could rely on transparency measures in place for another purpose. It is also possible to conclude treaties that are designed only to provide transparency and cooperation—as was the case with the 1992 Open Skies Treaty—without imposing any limits on forces and activities. And, just as nations could set their own level of force reductions, they could set their own level of transparency, for example, by publishing data periodically on the size of their forces or progress in reductions. Hence, there is no reason to assume, that, in the absence of a formal treaty, each party would lack all insights into the forces of the other.

Nevertheless, the absence of agreement on transparency measures, whether to monitor negotiated reductions or to account for unilateral adjustments, could undermine predictability. Not only might one or both nations choose to withhold information, but both sides could also lack the ability to confirm the veracity of the information. As a result, the information might do little to improve transparency. Even in an environment where the parties were willing to adjust their

---

[84] See, for example, U.S. Department of State, Bureau of Verification, Compliance, and Implementation, *Verification*, Fact Sheet, Washington, DC, April 8, 2010, http://www.state.gov/t/avc/rls/139906 htm.

forces unilaterally, without requesting or requiring reciprocity, a lack of accurate information about the other sides' forces could raise concerns.

At the same time, transparency may not always be a positive goal. For example, a nation may choose to adjust its forces unilaterally, rather than through negotiated limits, precisely because it does not want to provide access to information about its weapons. The government might believe that ambiguity regarding its nuclear arsenal may contribute to its deterrent value. A nation may also implement unilateral reductions in order to avoid providing critical national security information which might be necessary to verify compliance with treaty-mandated reductions. In such a case, the risks created by the intrusive monitoring needed to verify compliance with negotiated reductions may be greater than the benefits created by the predictability of balanced limits on the weapons. These considerations explain, in part, why the United States and Russia have never included limits on stored, nondeployed warheads in formal treaties, and why the United States has reduced this stockpile unilaterally over the years.

When President George H.W. Bush and President Gorbachev announced the PNIs in 1991, they did not include any cooperative monitoring measures in their proposals. The two nations could, to a certain degree, monitor the forces of the other nation with their own satellites and sensors— their national technical means (NTM) of verification. But they did not provide data on the numbers and locations of weapons covered by the PNIs, they did not notify each other when they planned to move those weapons, and they did not invite or permit inspections at storage or deployment areas. The United States and Russia have occasionally exchanged information on the progress of implementing the PNIs, and have provided some data on the status of their weapons. But this cooperation lacked the rigor of information required by arms control treaties. As a result, U.S. officials have occasionally raised questions about Russia's commitment to implementing the PNIs. Because they lack mechanisms to confirm or deny the accuracy of Russia's declarations, they do not have the same degree of confidence in Russia's compliance that they have with formal treaties.

At the same time, in an environment where the nations are willing to pursue unilateral reductions in their forces, incomplete knowledge about the other side's forces may not be a problem. For example, President George H.W. Bush stated in 1991 that he would withdraw U.S. land-based and sea-based nonstrategic nuclear forces from deployment regardless of whether the Soviet Union did the same. Therefore, although the United States probably would have liked precise information about the status of Soviet weapons, evidence that the Soviet Union (and Russia) had not followed through on its own withdrawals probably would not have affected the U.S. willingness to complete its reductions.

Similarly, President George W. Bush did not seek new transparency measures in the 2002 Moscow Treaty. When he presented the Moscow Treaty to the Senate, he indicated that the United States and Russia would continue discussions on transparency measures, and possibly add them to the treaty at a later date. But these discussions never occurred. It appears that, in 2001, the United States was willing to accept far less cooperation and shared information on nuclear weapons than it had sought in earlier years. This approach was consistent with the Administration's view that the United States and Russia were no longer enemies and that the United States no longer needed to size and structure its forces to counter a threat from Russia.

The Obama Administration offered a different view on the value of transparency in arms control. It indicated that one of the key reasons that it sought to negotiate a new Treaty with Russia in 2009 was to maintain the monitoring and verification capabilities of the 1991 START Treaty.

During the hearings on New START, Administration officials often highlighted the value of transparency and the New START monitoring regime in their statements in support of the treaty's ratification.[85] The Administration has also stressed its support for transparency and cooperation on nuclear weapons in its approach to possible limits on U.S. and Russian nonstrategic nuclear weapons. As was noted above, NATO, in its 2010 Strategic Concept, indicated that it would "seek to create the conditions for further reductions" in these weapons in the future. But it also indicated that, in any further reductions, NATO's "aim should be to seek Russian agreement to increase transparency on its nuclear weapons."[86] Moreover, in its 2012 Deterrence and Defense Posture Review, NATO indicated that, independent of reductions in nonstrategic nuclear weapons, the allies "look forward to continuing to develop and exchange transparency and confidence-building ideas with the Russian Federation" to increase "mutual understanding of NATO's and Russia's nonstrategic nuclear force postures in Europe."[87]

Timeliness

In most cases, it is likely to take far longer to reduce nuclear forces through a bilateral arms control treaty than it would to adopt unilateral adjustments to nuclear forces. First, it can take far longer to negotiate a treaty than to identify possible unilateral adjustments to nuclear forces. Second, it has, on many occasions, taken months or years for a treaty to enter into force after the conclusion of the negotiations, both because the legislatures must review and vote on the Treaty and because other domestic or international events intervene. Third, in some cases, the time lines for reductions included in treaties presume a slow and deliberate process, while the nations might be able to implement unilateral adjustments more quickly.

Negotiations

The United States and Soviet Union took over nine years to negotiate the original START Treaty. The talks opened in 1982. They stalled in the mid-1980s when the Soviet Union walked out after the United States deployed intermediate- range missiles in Europe. The negotiations resumed in earnest in 1985. They took another brief hiatus in early 1989, while the first Bush Administration reviewed U.S. arms control policy, and concluded in July 1991. In contrast, the George H.W. Bush Administration developed the list of measures for the 1991 PNIs in under a month.

These two examples represent the extremes. The United States and Russia took far less time to negotiate the second 1993 START II Treaty and the 2010 New START Treaty—they completed each in around one year. But both borrowed extensively from the original START Treaty. In addition, they completed the 2002 Moscow Treaty in four months, but this treaty contained simple aggregate limits and lacked any detailed definitions or monitoring provisions. Moreover, the George W. Bush Administration identified the limits codified in the treaty during a year-long Nuclear Posture Review in 2001.

---

[85] See, for example, the Statement of Admiral Michael Mullin, the Chairman of the Joint Chiefs of Staff, in U.S. Congress, Senate Foreign Relations, *The New START Treaty*, Hearing, 111th Cong., 2nd sess., June 15, 2010, S. Hrg. 111-738 (Washington: GPO, 2010), p. 48.

[86] North Atlantic Treaty Organization (NATO), *Active Engagement, Modern Defense*, Strategic Concept for the Defence and Security of the Members of the North Atlantic Treaty Organization, Lisbon, Portugal, November 20, 2012, p. 24, http://www nato.int/strategic-concept/pdf/Strat_Concept_web_en.pdf.

[87] North Atlantic Treaty Organization, *Deterrence and Defense Posture Review*, May 20, 2012, http://www nato.int/ cps/en/natolive/official_texts_87597 htm?mode=pressrelease.

Parties may slow formal negotiations in response to bilateral political difficulties, disputes over the details of the treaty, or other unforeseen events. Moreover, the negotiations may be unable to keep up with either the weapons-planning process or changes in the international environment.[88] For example, when the START negotiations began, the United States and Soviet Union were adversaries in a tense relationship. Two months after the nations signed the Treaty in 1991, President George H.W. Bush cancelled several weapons systems—such as the program to develop a mobile basing mode for the MX Peacekeeper missile and the program to develop a small single-warhead mobile ICBM—that would have been covered by the agreement. And six months after signing the Treaty, in December 1991, the Soviet Union ceased to exist. The parties then had to negotiate a Protocol to the Treaty, naming Ukraine, Belarus, Kazakhstan and Russia as successors to the Soviet Union under the treaty, before they could seek ratification of the treaty.

In contrast, unilateral measures, like those announced in the 1991 PNIs, might allow the United States (and Russia) to respond to sudden, unexpected changes in the international security environment because a unilateral, Presidential decision to alter U.S. nuclear forces is likely to be reached more quickly. With the PNIs, President George H.W. Bush sought analyses and alternatives from the Department of Defense and other agencies, but, without plans for formal negotiations, the U.S. government did not have to develop a negotiating strategy and fall-back positions. Similarly, in 2001, President George W. Bush expected to incorporate his planned reductions in U.S. nuclear weapons into his annual budget and DOD's policy guidance in a very short amount of time, without negotiating agreed definitions or balanced trades with Russia.

Entry into Force

Delays between the signing of a treaty and its entry into force are not inevitable. The United States and Soviet Union signed the 1972 Anti-Ballistic Missile (ABM) Treaty in on May 26, 1972; the Senate gave its advice and consent to ratification on August 3, 1972 and the treaty entered into force on October 2, 1972. However, several factors can lengthen the amount of time before arms control treaties enter into force. These include the time needed for the legislative body (both the United States Senate and the Russian Duma and Federation Council) to review and evaluate the terms of the treaty, international events that are either related or unrelated to the subject matter of the Treaty, and debates between the Administration and the Senate (or the Russian executive and Russian legislature) about issues related to, but not necessarily included in the framework of the Treaty.

The first of these factors, the length of time needed for debate in the legislature, is evident in all recent treaty histories. This would be expected for a lengthy or complex treaty, like the 1979 SALT II (Strategic Arms Limitation) Treaty and 1991 START Treaty. The Senate Foreign Relations Committee held more than two dozen hearings, over 5 months on SALT II. The Armed Services and Intelligence Committees also held hearings, leading to a total of 30 hearings, over 5 months. These three committees held 16 hearings, again over 5 months, on START in 1992. For the New START Treaty, in 2010, the Senate Foreign Relations Committee held nine hearings in 4 months, but the full Senate did not begin to debate the Treaty for an additional 6 months.

---

[88] For a discussion about the way the rapid changes in the international security environment interacted with the negotiations and implementation of the Conventional Armed Forces in Europe Treaty, see For a discussion of this type of "arms control trap," see Jeffrey D. McCausland, "Conventional Weapons, Arms Control, and Strategic Stability in Europe," in *Strategic Stability: Contending Interpretations*, ed. Elbridge A. Colby and Michael S. Gerson (Carlisle, PA: Strategic Studies Institute and U.S. Army War College Press, 2013), pp. 273-274.

International events can also slow or stop the arms control process. For example, the Soviet invasion of Afghanistan disrupted U.S.-Soviet relations and contributed to the failure of the 1979 SALT II Treaty. More recently, the break-up of the Soviet Union delayed the ratification of both the 1991 START Treaty and the 1993 START II Treaty. As was noted above, the parties negotiated a Protocol to START so that Ukraine, Belarus, and Kazakhstan could join Russia as successors to the Soviet Union for the Treaty. The parties signed this Protocol in May 1992. However, the Treaty could not enter into force until Ukraine, Belarus, and Kazakhstan agreed to return the nuclear warheads on their territories to Russia and joined the Nuclear Nonproliferation Treaty as non-nuclear nations. They completed this process, and START entered into force, on December 4, 2004, nearly 3.5 years after signature. Moreover, although the United States and Russia signed START II in January 2003, the U.S. Senate waited until START entered into force before beginning hearings on START II in early 1995. The Senate then delayed its vote on the treaty until January 1996. The Russian Duma also delayed its vote on the START II, in part due to concerns about U.S. missile defense plans and NATO enlargement.

The legislative debate on formal arms control treaties could also be delayed by debates between the executive and legislative branches on issues related to, but not covered within, the terms of the treaty. This was a key factor in the 1995 delay in the Senate's consideration of START II. The Senate Foreign Relations Committee held hearings on the Treaty in early 1995, but the Committee delayed its vote on the Treaty until early 1996 because of a dispute between the Clinton Administration and the Senate over the future of the Arms Control and Disarmament Agency. The Senate eventually consented to START II's ratification in January 1996. This was also evident during the Senate's consideration of the New START Treaty in 2010. The Treaty did not restrict weapons modernization; both sides could repair or replace existing weapons systems and the facilities that support those weapons. Yet the U.S. Senate spent a considerable amount of time seeking information from and negotiating with the Obama Administration about the amount of money it planned to allocate to nuclear modernization over the next decade.[89]

Unilateral adjustments in nuclear forces would not be exempt from legislative review. The House and Senate Armed Services Committees receive testimony on U.S. nuclear weapons plans and programs during the annual authorization and appropriations process. They could also call for separate oversight hearings if they wanted to review plans for unilateral adjustments in the U.S. nuclear arsenal. However, this would only slow the process of implementing reductions if Congress refused to appropriate necessary funds.

Implementation

Formal arms control treaties contain lengthy implementation periods that may not be present in unilateral measures. For example, the 1991 START Treaty allowed seven years for the parties to reduce their forces. Although they eliminated many weapons more quickly than mandated by the Treaty, neither the United States nor Russia completed their eliminations until the deadline of December 5, 2001. The 1993 START II Treaty, which, as noted, never entered into force, initially mandated that the United States and Russia complete their reductions by the beginning of 2003, 10 years after they signed the Treaty. But, in September 1997, after delays in the ratification process, the two nations agreed to extend the elimination period to the end of 2007. The 2002

---

[89] Elaine M. Grossman, "Offering Nuclear Plus-ups, White House Awaits Kyl's Word on "New START"," November 15, 2010.

Moscow Treaty allowed the parties 10 years to reduce their forces to agreed levels. The 2010 New START Treaty contains a seven-year reduction period.

In some cases, a long implementation process may be necessary because it can take a significant amount of time for the nations to comply with the detailed elimination procedures. Such a process also allows each nation to be certain that the other is meeting its obligations before it eliminates its own weapons. On the other hand, the lengthy time frame may add to the cost of nuclear weapons because the nations operate and maintain the forces for years even when they know they will eventually eliminate them. This factor has led some in the United States to argue that the United States should reduce its nuclear weapons to New START levels in fewer than the seven years permitted by the treaty. On the other hand, an accelerated drawdown schedule could also add costs if the Navy or Air Force have to build new facilities or assign added personnel to accommodate the new schedule.

Unilateral reductions can occur at whatever pace suits the needs of the nation adjusting its forces. They can occur slowly, as the George W. Bush Administration planned when it announced in 2001 that would reduce U.S. forces to between 1,700 and 2,200 warheads by 2012. They can occur quickly, as they did following the announcement of the PNIs in 1991. Or the pace can vary, as it has with reductions in the stored stockpile of nondeployed nuclear warheads, in response to decisions about the necessary size of the stockpile and the capacity of the system to process retired warheads.

Next Steps in Arms Control

Unilateral, Bilateral, or a Bit of Both

During its first term in office, the Obama Administration highlighted two objectives for its arms control policy. It wanted to reduce the number of nuclear weapons in the U.S. arsenal and it sought to do so in cooperation with Russia. It achieved these objectives with the signing and entry-into-force of the New START Treaty. President Obama and others in his Administration have indicated that the United States continues to support these two priorities. However, although the Administration has indicated that the United States would like to work with Russia to reduce nuclear weapons further, the Administration may not insist that the two nations codify these reductions in a formal, legally-binding treaty. The characteristics reviewed in this report can help explain why some support a possible shift away from formal treaties.

Balance and Equality

As was noted above, the 2010 NPR indicated that the United States preferred to maintain a measure of balance and equality between U.S. and Russian nuclear forces, but that absolute parity was not necessary. This supports a cooperative, reciprocal approach to arms reductions, but does not necessarily require that the parties negotiate a formal treaty that mandates strictly equal limits. At the same time, although the United States and Russia accepted equal limits on the number of strategic delivery systems and warheads in New START, the treaty permitted them to maintain significantly different strategic force structures[90] and far different numbers of nonstrateagic and

---

[90] The United States has more SLBMs warheads than ICBM warheads, and with a smaller number of warheads on each (continued...)

nondeployed nuclear warheads. In addition, each has different priorities for the types of forces and types of limits that they would like to include in a "next" arms control treaty. As a result, it would be difficult, and possibly time-consuming, for the United States and Russia to agree on the contents of a treaty that imposed balanced and equal limits on each side.

Predictability and Flexibility

During the Cold War, most U.S.-Soviet arms control treaties emphasized predictability over flexibility by incorporating limits on total forces, sublimits on specific types of weapons, restrictions on the locations and movement of limited systems, and precise definitions of items limited by the treaty. The 2002 Moscow Treaty emphasized flexibility over predictability because it contained no sublimits, no agreed definitions or rules to count the number of deployed strategic warheads, and no time frame for the reductions. The New START Treaty restored some of the predictability that had existed in the 1991 START Treaty, with agreed definitions on most systems limited by the treaty and with the exchange of detailed data on the status and numbers of deployed delivery systems. But it allowed far more flexibility than the original START Treaty as it allowed each side to determine its own mix of forces within the aggregate total.

If the United States and Russia agree to reduce their forces further while New START remains in force, they could rely on the definitions and monitoring provisions in New START to retain a degree of predictability and transparency. Those provisions will remain in force through at least 2021 or 2026, if they extend New START for five additional years. But they would increase their flexibility if they did not sign a new agreement that specified legally-binding limits. They would have the flexibility to size and structure their forces according to their own national security requirements and to restore forces if those requirements changed.

Transparency and Confidence in Compliance

The Obama Administration has indicated that it places a high value on the monitoring and verification provisions in New START and on the information they provide about the capabilities and numbers of nuclear weapons in Russia. They stated that the data exchanges, notifications, unique identifiers, and on-site inspections, provide each side with the ability to monitor strategic nuclear forces from "cradle to grave."[91] This would help both sides maintain confidence in the other side's compliance and agreement to pursue further reductions. On the other hand, the data exchanges and inspections in New START only apply to deployed strategic offensive forces and, in some cases, nondeployed strategic delivery vehicles. They do not provide any information about nonstrategic nuclear weapons or the stored stockpile of nondeployed weapons. Yet the Obama Administration has stated that the next round of arms control should include limits on these latter two categories of weapons.

If the United States and Russia agree to reduce their strategic nuclear weapons further, within the framework of New START and without negotiating a new treaty, they could rely on the

---

(...continued)

missile, a greater total number of delivery systems. Russia, in contrast, maintains more warheads per missile, and more land-based than submarine based missiles. See New START report for illustrative force structures.

[91] U.S. Congress, Senate Committee on Foreign Relations, □□e □e□ S□□□□ □reaty □reaty □oc□□□□□, Hearing, 111th Cong., 2nd sess., June 15, 2010, S.Hrg. 111-738 (Washington: GPO, 2010), p. 228.

monitoring and verification provisions in New START to provide transparency into the reductions. However, they would either have to leave nonstrategic and nondeployed weapons outside the framework of a new agreement or, if they counted them in the limits, they would have to accept less transparency about the numbers and locations of those weapons. Although either approach may achieve some U.S. goals for arms control—either deeper reductions in strategic nuclear weapons or reductions in all categories of weapons—neither would be as comprehensive and transparent as a formal treaty. In addition, this approach would not be consistent with NATO's stated goal of negotiating transparency measures that would provide insights into Russia's nonstrategic nuclear weapons.

Timeliness

Although the United States and Russia have taken preliminary steps to prepare for another round of arms control negotiations, there is widespread agreement that the formal arms control process has stalled. Russian officials have made it clear that they do not plan to move forward on further reductions in strategic offensive forces until the United States agrees to limit the eventual scope of its missile defense plans.[92] Further, they have argued that Russia would not negotiate limits on, or possibly even transparency measures for, nonstrategic nuclear weapons until the United States withdraws its nuclear weapons from bases in Europe.

Yet, the President and others in his Administration have stated that they believe the United States can achieve its deterrence and national security goals with a reduced number of nuclear weapons. Although the United States does not need to adjust its forces quickly, as it did in 1991, to respond to events such as the collapse of the Warsaw Pact and the abortive coup in Moscow, a near-term decision to reduce U.S. forces below New START levels could translate into budget savings if it allowed the United States to delay or scale back the planned modernization programs for these weapons.[93] At the same time, some in the Administration, and many in the arms control community, argue that continued, near-term steps to reduce the U.S. nuclear arsenal could help the United States win support from other nations in seeking to stem nuclear proliferation and strengthen the Nuclear Nonproliferation Treaty.[94]

The United States and Russia might agree to reduce their strategic nuclear weapons in parallel, without negotiating a new Treaty, so that they could avoid delays in implementation that might result from a lengthy debate in the Senate or the Russian parliament. While it is not inevitable that Senate or parliamentary consideration of a Treaty would delay or prevent the implementation of

---

[92] The Pentagon recently announced plans to cancel the fourth phase of the missile defense system that it plans to deploy in Europe. This phase, which would have been deployed after 2022, had caused Russia the greatest concern. Some observers have questioned whether this change in U.S. plans might soften Russia's opposition to further reductions in offensive weapons. Early reports from Russian officials indicate that this has not occurred. See David M. Herszenhorn and Michael R. Gordon, "U.S. Cancels Part of Missile Defense that Russia Opposed," *e or i es*, March 16, 2013; Desmond Butler, "Missile Plan Changes May Provide Opening for Talks," *ssociated ress* March 16, 2013; "Russian Diplomat: Moscow Unmoved by U.S. Missile Defense Change." *ssociated ress* March 18, 2013.

[93] For a description of the modernization programs planned for U.S. strategic nuclear weapons see Amy Woolf, "Modernizing the Triad on a Tight Budget," *r s Control oday*, January/February 2012. http://www.armscontrol.org/ act/2012_01-02/Modernizing_the_Triad_on_a_Tight_Budget. For an assessment of how changes in the modernization plan might reduce costs, see Arms Control Association, *clear eapons dget*, Fact Sheet, Washington, DC, March 18, 2013, http://www.armscontrol.org/files/FactSheet_Nukes_03_2013.pdf.

[94] Steven Pifer and Michael O'Hanlon, *e pport nity: e Steps in ed cing clear r s* (Washington, DC: Brookings Institution Press, 2012), p. 9.

---

reductions, recent history suggests that this is a possible, or even likely, outcome. In contrast, as happened in 1991 under the PNIs, the two sides could possibly begin to implement unilateral, parallel reductions in a very short amount of time.

Issues for Congress

Nature of the Commitment

If the United States and Russia agree to reduce their nuclear weapons below the levels in the New START Treaty without signing a new treaty, Congress may question whether the agreement represents a legal obligation or a political commitment, and whether the agreement is covered by the terms of the Arms Control and Disarmament Act. The answer to this question may depend on both the substance and the form of the agreement. If each nation simply announces, in a unilateral statement, that it plans to reduce its forces below the limits in New START, then this almost certainly would not represent a legally-binding obligation subject to congressional review and approval. Arguably, the unilateral statements would simply alter the manner in which the parties intend to implement the treaty. On the other hand, if the two nations sign an agreement that alters the limits in New START, this would be an amendment subject to the advice and consent of the Senate.

Between these two extremes, the United States and Russia could issue a joint statement or sign a shared memorandum of understanding incorporating the newly agreed levels for nuclear reductions. The question of whether the President should be required to seek Congressional approval for this type of agreement would likely rest on the substance of the agreement. If the two nations agreed that they would act as if they had changed the limits in New START, and did not specify that they viewed this change to be politically-binding only, then Congress may consider this agreement to represent a new legally-binding obligation for the United States. If it is treated as an amendment to the Treaty, then the Senate would have to offer its advice and consent, by a two-thirds vote, before it could enter into force. If it were treated as a congressional-executive agreement, both the House and Senate would have to vote to pass legislation that approved its limits. However, if the joint statement indicated that each side planned, on its own, to reduce its forces below New START levels, without changing the terms of the Treaty or adopting an obligation to complete the new, deeper reductions, then Congress may not have a role to play in approving the agreement. Congress could, however, limit funding for activities that would reduce the size of the force below a specified standard.

Priorities Among the Characteristics

If the United States and Russia agree to reduce their nuclear weapons below the levels in the New START Treaty, in parallel and without a formal Treaty, Congress may question whether the Obama Administration shares its priorities regarding the characteristics described above. For example, in choosing this path to further reductions while the two sides remained bound by the New START Treaty, the Administration would indicate that predictability and transparency remained important. Balance and equality would receive a lower priority while flexibility and timeliness would grow more important. Specifically, with this path forward, the two nations would decide for themselves how deeply and how quickly to reduce their forces without requiring strict equality and without consuming months or years in negotiations. In addition, they could begin to implement the reductions without seeking, and waiting for, the approval of their respective legislative bodies.

Some in Congress may support this ordering of priorities if, for example, they believe that deeper reductions in nuclear weapons might reduce the costs of these systems without undermining U.S. security. If the United States and Russia find it very difficult and time-consuming to find a balanced, equitable agreement that addressed all the issues that concern both sides, an informal understanding allowing each to move forward on its own could avoid this process. This could help the United States and Russia save money by eliminating the need to operate as many forces in the near term and to procure new replacement systems in the long term.

Others, however, may oppose this ordering of priorities, particularly if they see more risks than benefits to lower U.S. force levels. For example, some Members of Congress have stated that the United States should not rush to reduce its nuclear forces at a time when nuclear-armed countries like China, India, and Pakistan are not bound by arms control agreements. Moreover, some could argue that the United States should not pursue further reductions now, even if it has the flexibility to reverse the reductions in the future, when North Korea is increasing its nuclear arsenal and Iran is suspected of having a nuclear weapons program.[95] Finally, many in Congress may question whether it is necessary for the Administration to place such a high priority on timeliness when such a choice could leave Congress out of the arms control process.

Policy on Further Reductions

Debates in Congress over how to pursue further reductions in nuclear weapons may, in fact, be proxies for debates over whether the United States should pursue reductions at all. Specifically, some in Congress may support or oppose the mechanism chosen by Administration if it pursues further reductions because they support or oppose the goal of further reductions. Members who believe that the United States should reduce its nuclear weapons further might support that goal whether the United States codifies the limits in a formal treaty, pursues the reductions without a treaty but in parallel with Russia, or adjusts its forces unilaterally. Alternatively, Members who do not support further reductions in U.S. nuclear weapons may oppose such a policy regardless of whether the limits are codified in a treaty, outlined in mutual, nonbinding agreement, or implemented unilaterally. As a result, Congress may seek to pursue a debate that specifically addresses questions about the degree to which further reductions in nuclear weapons might serve to enhance or undermine U.S. national security.

Author Contact Information

Amy F. Woolf
Specialist in Nuclear Weapons Policy
awoolf@crs.loc.gov, 7-2379

---

[95] Bob Corker and Jim Inhofe, ""Nuclear Zero" Offers Nothing Worth Having," *Wall Street Journal*, February 26, 2013, p. A15.